D1429705

THE War Within

A Holistic Approach to Preventing Veteran Suicide

Krystle Shapiro, MSHN, LMT

Copyright © 2018 Krystle Shapiro, MSHN, LMT.

All rights reserved. No part of this book may be used or reproduced by any means, graphic, electronic, or mechanical, including photocopying, recording, taping or by any information storage retrieval system without the written permission of the author except in the case of brief quotations embodied in critical articles and reviews.

This book is a work of non-fiction. Unless otherwise noted, the author and the publisher make no explicit guarantees as to the accuracy of the information contained in this book and in some cases, names of people and places have been altered to protect their privacy.

The information, ideas, and suggestions in this book are not intended as a substitute for professional medical advice. Before following any suggestions contained in this book, you should consult your personal physician. Neither the author nor the publisher shall be liable or responsible for any loss or damage allegedly arising as a consequence of your use or application of any information or suggestions in this book.

The appearance of U.S. Department of Defense (DoD) visual information does not imply or constitute DoD endorsement.

LifeRich Publishing is a registered trademark of The Reader's Digest Association, Inc.

LifeRich Publishing books may be ordered through booksellers or by contacting:

LifeRich Publishing
1663 Liberty Drive
Bloomington, IN 47403
www.liferichpublishing.com
1 (888) 238-8637

Because of the dynamic nature of the Internet, any web addresses or links contained in this book may have changed since publication and may no longer be valid. The views expressed in this work are solely those of the author and do not necessarily reflect the views of the publisher, and the publisher hereby disclaims any responsibility for them.

Any people depicted in stock imagery provided by Getty Images are models, and such images are being used for illustrative purposes only. Certain stock imagery © Getty Images.

ISBN: 978-1-4897-1900-3 (sc)
ISBN: 978-1-4897-1899-0 (e)

Library of Congress Control Number: 2018910739

Print information available on the last page.

LifeRich Publishing rev. date: 09/29/2018

Dedication

I dedicate *The War Within* to my daughter Cydne Jenae Shapiro who taught me perseverance and faith in one's self to reach one's goals.

Acknowledgments

I am sincerely appreciative of the works by Dr. Sherry Rogers. Dr. Rogers researches and teaches environmental medicine and has published several books educating physicians as well as lay people interested in improving their health. The first book of hers I read was *Detoxify or Die* (2002). If it hadn't been for her, I never would have entered my studies at Hawthorn University as a master's of science in holistic nutrition student in February 2007.

Her passion to find the answers to overcoming environmental illness and her compassion to share all she discovered, uncovered, and practiced with her clients and with the interested public is most remarkable.

Her dedication to reflect the truth in medicine as to why the sick get sicker quicker, even against the naysayers and medical giants such as the American Medical Association and big pharmaceutical companies, must be respected and her knowledge followed in light of our present-day epidemic of chronic disorder and overall lack of wellness.

Thank you, Dr. Rogers, for providing such rich and appropriate medical information and for enlightening so many of us to share what we learn from you with others to turn the tide and experience enduring wellness.

I am very grateful for the assistance of two special friends who are savvy in computer technology who accomplished the specific details to prepare this book for publication. Sam McGlothlin reformatted all my charts into Word tables. Tari Pardini converted the photos into jpeg format. Thank you both for your invaluable help.

I also wish to thank all my friends and family who have supported my efforts to complete this book and maintain my confidence that I am presenting very useful information for healing our veterans and reducing the heartbreaking incidents of suicide among our beloved military personnel.

Contents

Humans owe their ascendance in the animal kingdom to their extraordinary capacity to adapt. Throughout evolution, humans have been exposed to terrible events, yet most people who are exposed to dreadful experiences survive without developing psychiatric disorders. Throughout history, some people have adapted to terrible life events with flexibility and creativity, while others have become fixated on the trauma and gone on to lead traumatized and traumatizing existences.

—Bessel A. Van Der Kolk and Alexander C. McFarlane: *Traumatic Stress: The Effects of Overwhelming Experience on Mind, Body, and Society*, (2007), p. 3

Introduction

The key to overcoming the rising rate of suicide in returning veterans from Iraq and Afghanistan must focus on replenishing critical and essential nutrients lost due to extreme and chronic toxic exposures in theaters of war that have a resounding effect on their health.

The increasing statistics of suicide each month by the Iraq and Afghanistan veterans returning from combat zones concern not only family, friends, and the military but also citizens around the world.

It has also become disturbing to learn that numbers are increasing for female veteran suicides and the incidence of suicide in older veterans. The VA's comprehensive report "Suicide Among Veterans and Other Americans, 2001—2014," published August 3, 2016, says that there is "the continued evidence of a high burden of suicide among middle-aged and older veterans. In 2014, about 65 percent of all veterans who died by suicide were ages 50 and older."

Theaters of war present extreme experiences of chronic stress: toxic exposures to aircraft and automotive fuels, ammunition residues, pesticides, herbicides, potential of extremes in climate temperatures, physical stress, constant noise, irregular hours for sleeping and eating, and highly processed foods prepared as MREs (meals-ready-to-eat) to carry with them. MREs have long-lasting shelf lives with many forms of preservatives, colorants, and flavor enhancers presently known to be unhealthy, not nourishing, and potentially carcinogenic. Understanding the long-term impact of such extreme chronic exposures and the nutritional remediation required to replenish lost body stores must be included in the current focus aimed at preventing suicide in returning veterans.

Chronic stress affects every system of the human body. Each system requires specific nutrients ingested regularly to manufacture the necessary hormone chemical messengers and enzymes required for proper cellular metabolism and for absorption of proteins, carbohydrates, and appropriate fats to nourish every cell in the human body. Whole foods supply these nutrients. When vital nutrients are deficient over a long period of time and body stores critically diminish, the organ systems of the body, such as the brain, the immune system, the gastrointestinal system, the adrenal system, and the urinary tract system, begin to weaken and break down. When this occurs, vital cellular communication enabling effective response and clear thinking processes also begin to deteriorate.

It is important to recognize also that influences on our bodies throughout our life experiences, physically, psychologically, and emotionally, are events our innate cellular system stores for reference for any time in the future we need to undertake that familiar fight-or-flight response. Just as this response can save us or lead to our doom, so do the microscopic cellular structures of our bodies store information to ensure our survival. Predation by outside influences, such as environmental toxins, unfamiliar chemicals, and such, plays a major role in health outcomes several years later in one's life. This understanding about cellular structure and cellular memory relates specifically to the recognition that older veterans, suffering from post-war memories, stored as experiences in their cellular structure, have experienced years of a cascade of natural stress chemicals for health maintenance that have become at some point finally exhausted, thus influencing brain function.

As the daughter of an Air Force veteran who served in WWII and Korea, I have been sensitive to the patriotic commitments and sacrifices of our soldiers and veterans throughout the years. Upon graduating summa cum laude with my master's of science in holistic nutrition, I felt a call to research the challenges our veterans face in combat zones and how nutritional intervention might play a dramatic part in health recovery upon their return.

I concluded my initial research in 2012, and many of the statistics presented in this book come from information gathered during that time. In the years following, the statistics varied little, and it was disappointing to try to find more updated information other than the controversy over the daily number of veteran suicides (from twenty-two a day reported by the VA in 2012 to twenty a day reported by the VA in 2016). The August 3, 2016 report by the Office of Suicide Prevention with the Veterans Administration provides comprehensive information about veteran suicide through 2014.

I still find little research by health care professionals associated with our government, our military departments, and other civilian agencies invested to recognize the underlying causes of this distressing and increasing occurrence of veteran suicide. Most attention has been on increasing the availability of mental health providers rather than looking into how the overall impact of toxic exposures and nutritional deficiencies experienced by our troops highly affect their brains and bodies systemically, thus causing a breakdown in communication transport and efficient and healthy functioning in the body. Of course maintaining a strong focus on mental health is critically important as well, as our soldiers have faced dramatic shifts in their lifestyles, expectations, and efforts to be a part of the solutions to resolve our current wars. Yet it must not be overlooked that human beings are living organisms impacted by their surroundings and exposures and respond positively or negatively through their belief systems, their interactions with others, their environment, their minds' and bodies' ability to adapt, and their opportunities to fuel their bodies optimally to think with clarity and to react with effective physical and mental abilities.

Krystle Shapiro
January 2018

The Heartbreak of Veteran Suicide

The rising numbers of suicide each month by the Iraq and Afghanistan veterans; the rising incidence of suicide by female veterans returning from combat zones; older veterans committing suicide; and incidents of noncombat veterans taking their lives concern not only families, friends, and the military but also American citizens supporting our societal philosophy of democracy and individual freedom. War veterans who have successfully survived the horrors of their deployment only to feel so damaged and unable to recover and reintegrate into their former lifestyles and who feel the need to kill themselves stateside cannot be overlooked. Our present military is comprised of volunteers from our American population. Recruitment in the future may become difficult if young men and women, eager to serve their country, begin to fear they may succumb to suicide upon their return (Harrell & Berglass, 2012; Wong, 2011).

Lack of Accurate Data on Suicide Numbers

Controversy exists in how data are collected about suicide statistics among all represented branches of service in Iraq and Afghanistan. But what may also be important in our understanding of the statistics, heartbreaking as they are, is to also understand some of the roadblocks to retrieving accurate figures of our soldiers committing suicide.

Dustin DeMoss, veteran, writer, and mental health warrior, posted in an update on March 7, 2015, for the Huffington Post (referring to the twenty-two-a-day statistic in 2012) that this number may not reflect the real number of daily suicides due to only twenty-one states in the United States reporting such statistics as veteran suicides due to a number of factors: family reluctance to reflect a death by suicide to preserve family memories, deaths by other means, such as accidents or provocations perpetrated by a veteran but leaving no notes for clarity, or by "the lack of a normalized and constant procedure [whereby there has been] no independent confirmation of such information with the Defense Department." This indicates the ongoing controversy of statistics gathering that may not represent realistic numbers of suicide deaths.

The current Department of Veterans Affairs report dated August 3, 2016, notes that twenty veterans a day commit suicide, down from twenty-two a day reported in 2012. This information states the VA looked at "55 million Veteran's records from 1979 to 2014 from every state in the nation" (Office of Public and Intergovernmental Affairs, *VA Releases Report on Nation's Largest Analysis of Veteran Suicide*, August 3, 2016).

The circumstances surrounding each suicide are as unique as the individuals themselves, and trying to sort out the dilemma for the military is difficult for many reasons. Many different studies continue to address such discrepancies in reporting with the hope of recognizing the depth of the suicide crisis and formulating a positive approach to developing a more comprehensive health-based plan for solution finding.

Kristina Wong in the November 2, 2011, report by CNAS (Center for a New American Security) indicates many factors as contributors to suicide, such as "lack of [enough] mental health care and behavioral health care professionals," lack of time between deployments, loss of support from one's unit upon return (a sudden loss of belonging), lack of understanding of a soldier's experience by new commanders when change occurs, and individuals returning with traumatic brain injuries. "Additional factors that heighten risk of suicide include chronic pain and post-traumatic stress disorder symptoms such as depression, anxiety, sleep deprivation, substance abuse, and difficulties with anger management." This report states "these factors are also widely associated with deployment experience in Afghanistan and Iraq" (Wong, 2011).

Recognition of the underlying symptomology leading to suicide includes the following states: depression, anxiety, addiction, emotional dysfunctions such as anger and rage, withdrawal from family and friends, mood changes, and a denial that problems exist. Other factors include frequent deployments, exposure to extreme stress factors, and "physical or sexual assault while in the military" as a few examples (Menna, 2011). Wong (2011) further adds the more commonly identified risk factors as "work-related problems, financial pressure, legal concerns, alcoholism and substance abuse."

For example, this certainly begins to identify the challenges faced by Army Staff Sargent Robert Bales, a veteran soldier blamed for executing sixteen civilians, most of whom were children, in an early morning foray in March 2012. News media reports indicate he felt extremely troubled by not having received an anticipated promotion. He faced his fourth deployment to Afghanistan, and he had deeply held concerns about resolving his family's financial troubles that stood to undermine their overall security. Sgt. Bales may have been a victim of extreme physiological toxicity making it impossible for him to think clearly and to process traumatic events into relevant new acceptances of reality to deal with his old lifestyle patterns upon his return to his family between deployments.

Prior to this incident, however, all branches of the military concerned themselves with the rising numbers of suicide and were focused on understanding the underlying multifactorial causes. Wong reports Army Deputy Chief of Staff Major General Thomas Bostick, testifying before a congressional hearing in Washington, DC, in September 2011 said:

It's very, very difficult to assess the effectiveness of the programs [suicide prevention programs]. I think some are very early, some are still in the progress of piloting and, because it's not one solution fits all, we really need to come at this at multiple levels from multiple directions. It is very, very complex.

This is good news for the nutrition depletion and replenishment argument that I address later on to become part of the discussion. In my initial 2012 research into the rising incidence of veteran suicide, I found very few references in military-focused articles and literature correlating multiple high toxicity exposures causing human nutrient depletion experienced by veterans in the combat zones as a potential cause for dysfunction within the brain and organ systems supporting healthy physical, emotional, and spiritual responses.

In 2016 the military research facility Natick Research Center and the USARIEM (US Army Research Institute of Environmental Medicine, Military Nutrition Division) presented many articles and videos finally addressing the importance of nutritional balance in prepared meals for combat soldiers in a variety of needs in the field, and they have developed First Strike Rations with higher nutrient content and lighter weight to assist soldiers carrying heavy packs while on missions. However, in view of the rising incidence of veteran suicide, these wonderful efforts have not mentioned toxic exposures, even from highly processed foods, as part of the contributors to brain dysfunction potentially leading to suicide at some point.

This ongoing research, understanding the physical demands of combat soldiers, must be put into the perspective of how deficiencies of the nutritional needs of the human body, caused by many toxicity factors depleting vital body nutrients, can alter how the brain determines its responses, especially during times of chronic stress and how such physical dysfunctions can lead to suicidal ideation and the potential for follow-through.

I believe it is also vital to one's understanding of a soldier's desire to commit suicide to recognize the interconnections of a soldier's prior lifestyle and environmental experiences that may contribute to disturbances in relevant thinking patterns. As laymen, we can understand the cognitive behavior theorists as they present a model of thought processes and beliefs that may serve as background and reasons for suicidal follow-through.

Briefly, as I understand this model, early experiences influence our core beliefs about ourselves, our being lovable and loving, of feeling okay and accepted, and of having purpose as we mature. If such experiences tend to be unhappy ones, these also influence our core beliefs that can lead to misperceptions of oneself, in turn leading to mood swings. This in turn again releases a cascade of chemical messengers in the human body to manage the stress. Prolonged experience of negative self-perceptions may lead to transference of negative views toward others, overgeneralizing, a growing sense of loss of purpose and hopelessness, and the potential for suicide.

Theaters of war present extreme experiences of chronic stress: toxic exposures to aircraft and automotive fuels, ammunition residues, pesticides, herbicides, potential of extremes in climate temperatures, physical stress, irregular hours for sleeping and eating, emotional stress, the stress of confrontation with the ideals and practices of other societies that may be in psychological opposition to the soldiers, and highly processed foods prepared as MREs (meals ready to eat) to carry with them. MREs have long-lasting shelf lives, translating into a high level of preservatives and flavor enhancers presently known to be unhealthy and non-nourishing, and they include some ingredients recognized as potentially carcinogenic, to be discussed later. Considering a person's emotional, psychological, and physiological history and understanding the long-term impact extreme chronic exposures present to human body health, nutritional remediation must be recognized as a vital requirement and a complementary strategy along with mental/behavioral health and pharmacotherapy.

Chronic Stress Causes Nutrient Deficiencies

As stated earlier, chronic stress affects every system of the human body. Each system requires specific nutrients ingested regularly to manufacture the necessary hormone and neurotransmitter chemical messengers and enzymes required for proper cellular metabolism and energy production. Whole foods supply these nutrients. When vital nutrients are deficient over a long period of time and body stores critically diminish, the organ and gland systems of the body, such as the central nervous system—including the brain, hypothalamus, and pituitary, as well as the thyroid gland, adrenal glands, immune system, gastrointestinal system, liver, urinary tract system, and cardiovascular system—begin to weaken and break down. When this occurs, vital cellular communication enabling effective responses and clear thinking processes also begin to deteriorate.

Human Body Experiencing Chronic Stress

The human body is a miraculous living organism teeming with synergistic interaction focused on survival. Just as humans marvel at the sometimes seeming impossibility of a fir tree establishing itself in a tiny crack in a sloped rock outcropping, so the human body establishes itself in an environment resplendent with wonderful opportunities as well as devastating consequences. Survival depends on many adaptations to one's environment as well as one's innate determination to survive.

The mystery of why some people in extreme conditions survive better than others must unravel itself around understanding the myriad interactions of the human body: recognizing its chemistry, its electrical output for energy, its metabolism, and its quest for high-quality incoming raw materials to sustain its survival instincts. And just as importantly, each person exhibits his or her own unique biochemistry through ancestral roots to present manifestations from lifestyle choices and exposures that play a role in reactions to extreme and/or traumatic experiences.

Stress abounds in all environments, whether human, animal, or plant based. It cannot be ignored, but it can be managed. If it is not managed, then adaptation or extinction will occur.

A quick review of cellular structures occurring throughout the human body provides an understanding of the importance of ingesting necessary nutrients essential for efficient and effective functioning during times of stress. A balanced whole foods diet ensures timely delivery of raw materials that enable vital brain functions as well as other important synergistic cellular/system interactions. Inadequate ingestion of essential nutrients can contribute to the development of depression, anxiety, panic disorder, aggression, rage, psychosocial behavior, suicidal ideation, and suicide follow-through, all conditions that trouble many veterans returning from combat in Iraq and Afghanistan (Wong, 2011).

The Brain, Amygdala, Hippocampus, Hypothalamus, Pituitary, and Adrenals

The human brain is responsible for making interpretations of what we experience from external and internal stimuli and formulating the appropriate cellular signaling chemistry to be forwarded to the next level of response. This remarkable organ is "nearly 60% fat. The fats and oils ingested shape the brain's fatty acid architecture" (Schmidt, 2007, p. xv). This becomes important to understand what can undermine cellular signals leading to miscues and improper mental/emotional responses in times of stress as well as to be aware of lingering stress interpretations.

Cellular membranes are responsible for many functions, such as providing flexible sites for various receptors that transport nutrients into cellular matrices for the production of energy as well as release cellular wastes for elimination. Such flexibility is made possible by the membrane's structure composed of fatty acids. Saturated fatty acids as well as unsaturated fatty acids in the forms of monounsaturated and polyunsaturated fatty acids comprise cellular membranes. Saturated fats provide strength and stability to cell membranes, and mono and poly unsaturated fats provide flexibility. Even though our society fears certain fats, like saturated fats, these are important for the proper functioning of cellular membranes within the body and especially in the brain.

Ingestion of too much of one type of fatty acid alters the composition of cellular membranes throughout the body, rendering them either too stiff or too soft and thereby debilitating receptor sites from effective energy transport into cellular matrices or transporting wastes and cellular debris out of and into the interstitial fluids for transport by the immune system for elimination. Ingestion of too many "bad fats" is an example of disruption of cellular membrane activity. These fats, called trans fats, which area found in most grocery store brands, are highly processed hydrogenated fats and oils molecularly transformed in processing that have a negative health effect on the body known to lower good cholesterol and potentiate cardiovascular conditions (University of Maryland Medical Center, November 3, 2010). As well, such fats can actually fit partway into receptor sites, clogging entrance by good fats and nutrients, but cannot provide the transport functions necessary for cellular metabolism.

A balance of fatty acids nurturing and feeding brain function enables the brain to formulate its chemical messengers called neurotransmitters. When a call to action occurs, such as illness, chemical toxins, overabundance of free radicals, or any other stressor, "fatty acids are released from the membrane and are chemically transformed into highly active hormone-like substances ... [that] exert powerful and profound effects on a vast array of functions within the brain" (Schmidt, 2007, p. 28).

The Human Body's Response to Stress

Outlining the neuroanatomy response cascade in times of stress provides the background for understanding the importance of vital nutrients in supporting the stress response by all body systems and for returning the human body to homeostasis when the crisis has subsided. This becomes especially important for addressing the psychological and physiological needs of returning veterans who are reintegrating into their former life patterns still heightened by the cellular and emotional memories of their combat/wartime experiences.

As stated earlier, the human brain receives stimuli/information and forms an interpretation. In a crisis situation, communication begins by notifying the hypothalamus just above the brainstem to set in motion a stress response. The hypothalamus secretes a hormone, corticotropin releasing hormone (CRH), that notifies the pituitary gland to initiate "a heavily regulated stress response pathway" (Wikipedia, 2012a). Part of this response involves the amygdala, a small structure located deep within the brain with "projections to and from the hypothalamus, hippocampus, and locus coeruleus ... The amygdala has been implicated in modulating stress response mechanisms, particularly when feelings of anxiety or fear [are] involved" (Wikipedia, 2012a).

The pituitary gland, upon receiving CRH, releases adrenocorticotropic hormone (ACTH). This hormone alerts the adrenal glands to release their hormones, especially cortisol, to manage major stress by redistributing the flow of energy to meet the needs for fight or flight, such as revving up the flow of glucose to muscles for quick action, increasing oxygen intake through more rapid breathing and increasing heart rate, and slowing down metabolism, immune response, sexual response, and any other functions that are unimportant when a major threatening event occurs.

Another brain participant in the stress response is the hippocampus, which is important in the formation of memories.

The hippocampus is particularly important in that cognitive processes such as prior memories can have a great influence on enhancing, suppressing, or even independently generating a stress response. The hippocampus is also an area in the brain that is susceptible to damage brought upon by chronic stress. (Wikipedia, 2012a)

This seems to be important information as to how war memories (flashbacks) can trigger a perceived stress situation when none truly exists, potentially leading to an aggressive response.

The liver plays a major role as it manages detoxification for the body, removing environmental and cellular toxic chemicals, cleansing the blood by metabolizing medications and excess hormones, as well as distributing and/or storing nutrients from dietary ingestion, among many other physical responsibilities. This liver activity helps maintain energy levels, support body functions, and improve brain functions (Stone, 2006). However, the liver can "be severely damaged by exposure to environmental toxins, drugs, and alcohol abuse" (Stone, 2006, p. 6). Stone further itemizes additional major threats to liver health, like poor water quality, poor nutrition, pollution, disease, and chronic stress.

Physiological Breakdown Leading to Depression and the Potential of Suicide

As evidenced by the above descriptions of the interactions of the hypothalamus, the pituitary, and the adrenal glands, referred to as the H-P-A axis, one can begin to understand the importance of proper cellular signaling to all systems of the body for optimal functioning, especially in times of extreme stress that combat scenarios present. For these systems to complete their intention to prepare the body for fight-or-flight responses, the vital nutrients required must first be metabolized efficiently by the digestive system. Without effective digestive absorption, no amount of good, clean food will support brain and organ activities.

The gastrointestinal (GI) tract carries out three important roles in maintaining an optimum brain-immune connection. First of all, the brain absolutely depends on the GI tract's ability to assimilate and deliver nutrients which act as essential building blocks for neurotransmitters. Secondly, the brain requires the GI tract to remove toxins which have the potential to adversely affect brain-immune function. And, finally, optimum brain health rests on the GI tract's ability to properly regulate immune system activity. (Lombard & Germano, 1997, p. 26)

Therefore, message transmission depends upon neurotransmitters, hormones, and flexible cellular membranes and especially myelin sheaths around neurons that insulate and enable message transmission, all relying on and supported by efficient GI tract metabolism of ingested nutrients that of themselves support digestive functions.

These key players in optimal functioning in times of stress, the hypothalamus, pituitary, adrenals (the H-P-A axis) along with the thyroid, liver, and gastrointestinal tract, all closely associated with the immune system, require optimal nutrition to function properly. When nutrient ingestion is altered, the cascade of information transmission throughout the body alters.

For example, the hypothalamus "links our emotions to our bodily responses … anger, depression, and anxiety are all mediated by chemical communication signals that originate in the hypothalamus" (Lombard & Germano, 1997, p. 10). The hypothalamus monitors and regulates vital internal conditions, such as body temperature, nutrient levels, water-salt balance, blood flow, the wake/sleep cycle, and levels of circulating hormones and "mediates the responses to emotions such as anger and fear" (Clayman, 1995, p. 77). The hypothalamus activity is supported by green vegetables as well as colorful vegetables containing beta carotenes, such as carrots, yams, kale, spinach, collard greens, dark colored lettuces, and butternut squash (HealthAliciousNess.com, 2011), by essential fatty acids found in several fish varieties, such as salmon, tuna, and mackerel, and essential oils like borage oil, flaxseed oil, fish oil, and proteins and oils found in seeds and nuts. These foods also provide essential minerals, such as potassium, magnesium, and manganese, all supporting hypothalamic activity.

The pituitary gland is extremely sensitive to diet, requiring enough high-protein foods, especially meats rich in essential amino acids, to produce its hormones (Braun, 2011). Good sources of proteins also come from plants. According to August McLaughlin (2011), "Eating too much animal protein in the form of meat, eggs, and dairy products can offset your hormone levels and increase your risk for problems related to your pituitary." McLaughlin (2011) also suggests including beans, lentils, and nuts, such as almonds for balancing protein intake supporting the pituitary gland. Vitamin A found in milk, liver, cod, eggs, and halibut (Kalmus, 2011), vitamin E richly found in wheat germ (Braun, 2011), and the mineral manganese found in citrus, whole grains, leafy greens, egg yolk, and all fish (Braun, 2011) are also needed to synthesize pituitary hormones. "If these nutrients are lacking, the pituitary will not function properly and neither will the rest of the glandular system" (Rohrer, 2012). One challenge Rohrer continues to emphasize highlights the fact that many proteins consumed are "devitalized," that is the amino acids have been altered by refining, processing, and improper high-temperature cooking.

The thyroid gland also relies on proteins for healthy functioning. "The thyroid gland is … closely linked with the normal functioning of all other glands in [the] body" (Braun, 2011). This small gland located at the front of the neck regulates the amount of oxygen consumption, secretes hormones regulating emotions, weight, skin and hair quality, and "stimulates [one's] sexual powers" (Braun, 2011). High-quality proteins as well as adequate iodine from sea foods, along with an array of vitamins and minerals from seeds such as sunflower seeds and pumpkin seeds providing B vitamins, magnesium, manganese and zinc, and grains such as whole wheat, buckwheat, and millet, providing B vitamins, manganese, iron, as well as fiber (Whole Grains Council, 2012) provide the thyroid with many of its essential requirements (Braun, 2011).

The adrenal glands respond to incoming stress signals from the pituitary. A person's "resiliency, energy, endurance, and [one's] very life all depend on their proper functioning" (Lam, Schmidt, & Wilson, 2012). The human body has a great capacity to manage stress long term, but without replenishment of necessary nutrients to formulate its secretions, the adrenals can become overworked, overtired, and exhausted. The adrenals operate best when supplied with whole foods and fresh vegetables with their full complement of vitamins and minerals, especially potassium, calcium, magnesium, and vitamins A and C and the vitamin B complex family.

Dr. Lam, et.al. (2012), itemizes four major categories of stress:

1. Physical stress: overusing the body through work, play, or lack of sleep;
2. Chemical stress: exposures to environmental pollutants, highly processed and refined diets, allergies, food additives, imbalances within the endocrine system;
3. Thermal stress: exposures to high heat or extreme cold;
4. Emotional and mental stress: these create a chemical cascade as well in the body.

General Adaptation Syndrome Response to Chronic Stress

A further step in understanding the negative cascade of emotional demise, possibly leading to suicide, Doctors Lam, et al. explain the three stages of the General Adaptation Syndrome (GAS) response to stress. Simplified here but important for understanding how GAS affects returning veterans may provide insight to the often-experienced delays in veterans reporting physical or psychological problems and seeking help.

First, the alarm reaction is received by the adrenal glands, and cortisol is released into the blood stream. This prepares the body for fight or flight, as defined earlier. Generally this reaction manages the stressor; then when the danger passes and heightened awareness and emotions subside, the hypothalamus, through an important feedback loop, retracts its order for secretions, cortisol levels recede, and homeostasis returns.

Second, the resistance stage may emerge whereby the danger is longer lasting than normal, either real or imagined, and a person begins to adapt to the pressure and physical requirement to manage the ongoing stressor. The biochemical reaction is thus: "The prolonged alarm reaction starts as a hyperadrenia [overactive adrenal output] which leads to a hypoadrenia [underactive adrenal output] which then progresses into another state of hyperadrenia as the resistance stage takes over" (Lam, et al. 2012, p. 2). This occurs because the body, in its wisdom, finds extra needed resources in tissue and bone stores. However, these stores are finite if they are not replenished regularly with vital nutrients.

"This phase of resistance can last months or even up to 15-20 years" (Lam, et.al, 2012, p. 2). This fact may be an important component of the biochemical breakdown potentially leading to suicidal ideation in returning veterans or their delay in seeking help. They may retain thoughts that might be interfering with their present-day stateside interactions; suffer from PTSD; have unresolved or newly developed family issues; have new health issues compromising their ability to work, play, or interact with others; or have feelings of lost personal worth or opportunities. Such new emotions on top of wartime ones adds to the continual cascade of negative hormone secretions.

Cortisol, Dr. Lam, et al., (2012), explains,

> is largely responsible [for stimulating] the conversion of proteins, fats, and carbohydrates to energy through gluconeogenesis [a system to generate other sources of glucose necessary for energy by taking raw materials from tissue and bone storage] so that [the] body has a large supply of energy long after glucose stores in the liver and muscles have been exhausted.

When the stress becomes severe or prolonged, the adrenal glands break down so that they can no longer manage the resistance stage, can no longer adapt or manage the ongoing stress, and begin to shut down into the third stage of the general adaptation syndrome: the exhaustion stage.

At this point, the body becomes weakened, an inadequate amount of energy is produced, and several cellular imbalances occur. The ongoing or accumulated stresses disable the adrenal glands from recovering. This can lead to electrolyte imbalances, hypoglycemia, fatigue, frustration, and an inability to self-motivate.

Depression—a Natural Outcome from Nutrient Depletions

The signs of depression are as varied as individuals as each person makes interpretations about their life experiences and judges them as beneficial or as sad liabilities. Depression may be of short duration whereby a person understands the situation and seeks either effective coping strategies or significant mental/emotional therapy, leading to a sense of resolution, or depression can evolve into a chronic state that can become life threatening. "Depression rarely exists alone ... patients often have lack of energy or fatigue as a major part of their depression, in addition to anxiety or phobias or fears" (Rogers, 1997a, p. 16).

There may also be physical symptoms, such as digestive disorders or a variety of body aches and pains. Emotional dysfunction may include "feelings of guilt and worthlessness, agitation, irritability, memory defects, inability to concentrate, difficulty in thinking and making decisions, or thoughts of death and suicide" (Rogers quoting Massarelli, 1997a, p. 17).

Research by Lombard & Germano (1997) found "that depression is closely linked to the dysfunction of two neurotransmitters in the brain [norepinephrine (p. 14) but] particularly serotonin" (p. 197). While pharmaceutical companies rushed to manufacture drugs effective in preventing the reuptake of serotonin, Lombard & Germano report as of 1997 that "about fifteen percent of people with this disorder commit suicide as a result" of not receiving treatment in time (p. 197). The question then arises: Is suicide an outcome of serotonin deficiency requiring drug intervention, or does some glitch occur in biophysical and chemical pathways that need nutrient remediation to properly function?

As we have learned from the previous discussion, the organ and glandular systems responsible for optimal functioning require high-grade raw materials to complete their hormonal secretion transactions. Deficiencies at any place along the communication pathways alter brain chemistry, and this can lead to changes in moods, behavior, and thought processing.

Importance of Essential Fatty Acids in Maintaining Mental Health

Essential fatty acid deficiency has been recognized as a major contributing factor to the onset of depression. The reason for this focuses on the brain's requirement for fatty acids in its cell structure that enables interactions between its chemical messengers, the neurotransmitters, and binding to their receptors. The most important fatty acids are the Omega-3s, especially the forms of DHA (docosahexaenoic acid) and EPA (eicosapentaenoic acid), as they ensure that norepinephrine and serotonin, two brain neurotransmitters associated as a safeguard against depression, properly bind to their receptor sites (Lombard & Germano, 1997).

These two authors further itemize causes of depression stemming from a genetic predisposition; faulty neurotransmitter function; low levels of tryptophan, which is a precursor to the happy hormone serotonin;

overproduction of CRH by the hypothalamus, leading to overproduction of cortisol by the adrenals (which in turn could mean adrenal exhaustion); and vitamin deficiencies such as riboflavin (B2), pyridoxine (B6), folic acid, and vitamin C (1997).

Schmidt (2007) agrees with these findings and states "If the right fats are not supplied, brain structure is altered. If brain *structure* changes, *function* changes" (p. 9). Most people today consume more animal fats from a high-meat diet; ingest many highly processed and refined foods manufactured at high heat temperatures using vegetable oils high in trans fats, an altered and degraded fat previously defined, as well as seasoned with flavor enhancers, additives, colorants, artificial flavors, sweeteners, and texturizers; and tons of sugary foods, disrupting insulin and blood glucose balances. This type of diet consumed regularly "is not at all conducive to building a complex, superbly functioning brain and nervous system. This may be the common feature that underlies a host of behavioral, learning, memory, and neurological disorders" (Schmidt, 2007, p. 9). Recognizably, a strong military force must be also prepared for extremely stressful combat situations, not only by physical prowess, but also by vital mental and emotional alertness and must be fed appropriately to meet the stringent requirements of their assignments.

Schmidt (2007) reports in his research findings that improper fatty acids and phospholipids (plant-based fats) have been associated with many types of brain disorders including aggression, anxiety, chronic fatigue, phobia (fears), rage, depression, drug abuse, hostility, self-mutilation, suicide, and/or violence. This information adds to the importance of providing rich, nutrient-dense whole foods full of vitamins, minerals, amino acids, enzymes, and proper fats and oils as part of any mental health recovery plan but especially pertinent in addressing any nutrient depletion status of returning veterans.

Deborah Brauser, reporting for Medscape on August 26, 2011, quotes from her interview with Dr. Joseph R. Hibbeln, a co-principal investigator and acting chief, Section on Nutritional Neurosciences at the National Institute on Alcohol Abuse and Alcoholism, National Institutes of Health, that his "findings add to an extensive body of research that points to a fundamental role for DHA and other omega-3 fatty acids in protecting against mental health problems and suicide risks." The study investigators further pointed out "the recent escalation of U.S. military suicide deaths to record numbers has been a sentinel for impaired force efficacy and has accelerated the search for reversible risk factors." They recognize that "omega-3 essential highly unsaturated fatty acids ... especially DHA are needed for optimal neural function" noting also that "suicide rates in military personnel have doubled since the start of Operation Enduring Freedom (OEF) and Operation Iraqi Freedom (OIF), and now 'rival the battlefield in toll'" (2011). This becomes shocking news for families and communities at home. Holistic nutritionists understand the dynamic impact whole food nutrition has on not only brain health but also on overall physical body health and mental well-being and the need for this information to be included along with all concepts being considered by investigative panels seeking solutions for the rising suicide crisis in the military.

As the concern about rising suicide rates climbs, studies continue. Zukier, Solomon, and Hamadeh (2011) report in their research that

> Epidemiological studies have found ... differences in diet (specifically in the consumption of fruits and vegetables, meat, fish, and fat) and in serum levels of essential fatty acids (EFA) and total cholesterol among those who have attempted suicide compared with people who have not. Persons with lower levels of serum cholesterol were found to have a greater risk of carrying out suicidal acts than those with higher levels.

Dr. James M. Greenblatt, reporting for *Psychology Today* in an article published September 3, 2011, "Nutritional Risk Factors for Suicide," also agrees with the now multiple studies and findings of the importance of ingesting essential fatty acids, especially omega 3 fatty acids rich in DHA. His report highlights a study reported in the Journal of Clinical Psychiatry, "Suicide Deaths of Active-Duty US Military and Omega-3 Fatty Acid Status: A Case-Controlled Comparison" and states the findings that servicemen with the lowest range of DHA levels were 62% more likely to have completed suicide than those with higher levels of DHA. It should be noted that all military personnel in the study [800 men and women who committed suicide and 800 matched personnel with no suicide attempt history] generally had low levels of DHA.

Magnesium Deficiency Linked to Suicide

Another dietary concern correlated to the rising incidence of suicide focuses on low magnesium consumption. Magnesium plays many important roles in the body: "at a biochemical level, more than 325 enzymes are Mg [magnesium] dependent, many of which are nervous system enzymes" (Cuciureanu & Vink, 2011).

Magdalena D. Cuciureanu and Robert Vink, 2011, state, Mg is the fourth most abundant cation [positively charged ion] in the body ... It is involved in a wide variety of cellular processes including aerobic (utilizing oxygen) and anaerobic (non-oxygen utilizing) metabolism, all bioenergetic reactions, regulation of metabolic pathways, signal transduction and many other cellular functions. Stress plays a major factor in the utilization of magnesium within the body "but extended periods of stress result in progressive Mg deficit and deleterious consequences for health" (Cuciureanu, et al., 2011 quoting Selig, 1994).

Proper levels of magnesium help alleviate fatigue. Fuchs (2002) itemizes the benefits of magnesium as providing regulation to nerve cell functions supporting relaxation, lowering sensitivity to loud noises, improving mood, and sleep patterns. "Magnesium, along with vitamin B6, helps produce serotonin, an important neurotransmitter" (Fuchs, 2002, p.52). "All kinds of stress contribute to excessive magnesium loss" (Fuchs,

2002, p. 25). Excessive adrenal output experienced in chronic stress causes magnesium to be excreted in urine (Fuchs, 2002).

The question arises as to what could be the causes of magnesium loss in our current dietary practices that potentiate depression and suicide or at least define occurrences in theaters of combat that contribute to the problem of magnesium loss. "Dietary magnesium intake has steadily declined over the preceding century" (Eby, Eby, & Murck, 2011). Such practices as highly refined grains; processing of many food products with high-heat techniques; and feeding animal food products unnatural feeds for their species and/or feeding foods highly treated with antibiotics, growth hormones, pesticides, and herbicides to animals to be consumed as food are well-known modern practices. As well, many people succumb to marketing glitz and may make dietary choices of foods low in magnesium such as processed or poorly fortified foods. "Extensive marketing and resultant consumption of excitotoxic glutamates and aspartates [that enhance flavor] have very greatly increased" (Eby, et al., 2011, quoting Blaylock, 1999; Walton et al., 1993). Glutamates (MSG) and aspartates (aspartame) are present in the MREs (meals ready-to-eat) provided to soldiers in combat zones and also may be present in other foods available in war zone operational kitchens. Cumulatively, consuming poor-quality foods contributes to magnesium loss by continual stress to digestive processes requiring natural nutrients to properly function.

The importance of magnesium in the diet and to brain health and the ongoing studies focused on understanding this correlation with suicide has become an important step toward defining effective nutritional interventions to overcome the present dilemma of rising suicides in returning veterans.

As well, understanding the fundamental biochemical and neurochemical interactions of the human body becomes vitally important as a foundation for understanding possible contributing factors to suicidal ideation and follow-through by veterans. High consumption of unnatural food products, such as highly refined and processed foods as well as prepackaged foods containing many chemical additives and flavor enhancers that promote long shelf life but are unnatural to health, contribute to a deterioration of optimal health. Over a long time, such ingredients can be damaging to brain chemistry and ultimately to the H-P-A axis organs' cellular signaling activities that require whole food raw materials, as described earlier.

However, a lack of nutrient-rich foods with balanced fats, proteins, and carbohydrates and ingestion of a variety of fresh fruits, vegetables, whole grains, meats, and seafood providing essential nutrients does not represent the only problem creating concern for the rising incidence of suicide in wartime veterans.

Additional Relevant Toxicity Factors: Toxic Exposures Existing in War Zone Military Operations

Soldiers in a combat zone are captive participants who have to undergo patrols and missions; maintain all necessary operations from food management and cooking, automotive and aircraft mechanical upkeep, and ammunition control; address medical needs for the wounded; take care of their own personal needs; and be ready at any given moment to interact with other soldiers for all daily activities. Their daily toxic exposures can reach such high concentrations that it is no wonder the detoxification pathways and adrenal hormones struggle to keep up, maintain, and endure such an onslaught.

Specific Military Toxins

Jet Fuels

Consumer Support Group, Inc. (CSG, 2012) provides information on aviation fuels and additives. Military jet fuels consist of Jet Propellent-4 (JP-4), JP-5, and JP-8 containing naptha and kerosene fractions and corrosion inhibitors, along with de-icing additives. Other additives include anti-knock additive, tetra-ethyl lead (TEL), anti-oxidant compounds, static dissipater additives, biocide additives to combat microbiological growths in the fuel, and power-boosting fluids such as methanol/water mixtures (CSG, 2012).

According to the Material Safety Data Sheet provided by Sciencelab.com (2012), kerosene is toxic to the nervous system. The substance may be toxic to blood, kidneys, liver, central nervous system (CNS). Repeated or prolonged exposure to the substance can produce target organs damage. Repeated exposure to a highly toxic material may produce general deterioration of health by an accumulation in one or many human organs.

Tetra-ethyl lead, while being banned in the US between the "late 1990s to early 2000s because of concerns over air and soil pollution … TEL remains an ingredient of 100 octane avgas for piston engine aircraft" used by aviation (Wikipedia, 2012e). It is important to note that "as of June 2011 … the only countries in which leaded gasoline is the only type available are … Afghanistan … [and] Iraq" (Wikipedia, 2012e), as well as many other Middle Eastern and Asian countries. This same article continues to explain the toxicity risk arising from lead poisoning, especially from engine exhaust [that is] dispersed into the air and into the vicinity of roads and easily inhaled … Lead is a toxic metal that accumulates and has subtle and insidious neurotoxic effects especially at low exposure levels, such as … antisocial behavior.

And further notation by Wikipedia authors that may be important in understanding any form of mental deterioration in returning veterans states "a statistically significant correlation has been found between the usage of leaded gasoline and violent crime" (2012).

Gasoline

Fuel-Testers (2012) states that gasoline contains "150-1000 different compounds and ethanol is just one of many." Just listing a few with more familiar names, gasoline also contains naptha, n-butane, benzene, toluene, and dyes. Naptha can cause "nonspecific depression of the central nervous system" as well as have a negative effect on "eyes, skin, [respiratory system, central nervous system], liver, [and] kidney" (Wikipedia, 2012c). The Material Safety Data Sheet provided by *Airgas* (2012) states that n-butane "may cause damage to the … central nervous system." Wickedroots.com (2006) further clarifies the toxic effects of n-butane inhalation to include "dizziness, hypertension, increased heart rate, impaired coordination, disorientation … assaults, and suicide attempts."

The ATSDR (Agency for Toxic Substances & Disease Registry) (2012) states that benzene is "known to be a human carcinogen." Benzene is also a "natural part of gasoline and cigarette smoke." The Environmental Bureau of Investigation (EBI) (2012) states that "inhalation of benzene for long periods may cause harmful effects in the tissues that form blood cells, especially the bone marrow." Other effects include "dizziness, sleepiness, convulsions, rapid heart rate … and may also be harmful to the reproductive organs" (EBI, 2012).

Ethanol, a constituent of gasoline, also affects the central nervous system as a depressant. "Ethanol binds to acetylcholine, GABA, serotonin, and NMDA receptors" (Wikipedia, 2012b). These represent brain chemical messengers known as neurotransmitters. NMDA receptors, "a glutamate receptor, is the predominant molecular device for controlling synaptic plasticity and memory function" (Wikipedia, 2012d). Without proper and efficient synaptic activity (a chemical interaction between nerve junctions enabling message transmission and the processing of nerve impulse signals), challenges to mental, emotional, and physical responses can occur due to the failure of appropriate follow-up interactions by affected glands and organ systems.

Toluene also affects the central nervous system. Toluene may be inhaled from auto exhaust (ATSDR, 2012). Heller (2010) reports that toluene creates the following challenges to the body: gastrointestinal disturbances, kidney damage, breathing difficulties, nervousness, and blurred vision, to name a few that particularly may affect soldiers in combat zones.

While these toxins may be only small amounts within these fuels, the daily inhalation of fumes from aircraft, Humvees, tanks, and even cigarette smoke can have a cumulative effect that needs to be detoxified by already overloaded liver, adrenal, and immune systems from long-term daily stress. Detoxification requires vital natural nutrients ingested daily to be effective in supporting health.

Noise

Another toxic exposure in combat zones, one we don't often think of as toxic, is noise. "Chronic low level noise negatively influences the brain and behavior" according to the Franklin Institute (2004) referencing Dr. Alice H. Suter, an audiologist at the National Institute for Occupational Safety and Health, with outcomes including "suicide and degradation of the immune system … in noise related problems" (p. 8). The constant din of aircraft, Humvees, tanks, radios, explosives such as IEDs (improvised explosive devices), mortars, and rockets, small arms, screams from panicked civilians, and screaming orders from commanders and unit leaders over the ongoing noisy output of combat zone activities all accumulate as noise stress toxicity, possibly even interrupting restful breaks and sleep times.

Burn Pits

Alarming information has arisen about burn pits in Iraq and Afghanistan exposing soldiers to toxic fumes from the burning of "discarded human body parts, plastics, hazardous medical material, lithium batteries, tires, hydraulic fluids, and vehicles. Jet fuel keeps pits burning twenty-four hours a day, seven days a week" (Garcia, 2011). The above discussion of the effects of components in fuels used in theaters of war on health cannot be ignored as these pits continue to be utilized. Garcia further reports in this article that,

The VA states that "chemicals, paint, … metals, aluminum, unexploded ordinance, munitions, and petroleum products among other toxic waste" are destroyed in burn pits. Possible side effects, the department notes, "may affect the skin, eyes, respiration, kidneys, liver, nervous system, cardiovascular system, reproductive system, peripheral nervous system, and gastrointestinal tract." (Garcia, 2011)

To date, many of the burn pits have been discontinued and have been replaced with incinerators that produce much lower toxicity, However, claims are increasing for respiratory health problems, challenges with vision, skin irritations, glandular and digestive disorders, and cancers by veterans having served in these wars over the years who exhibited no such conditions prior to deployment. An online search titled "Respiratory claims by veterans" listed several sites such as Alphadisability.com reporting that "disability claims continue to mount up (regarding open burn pits) … The Department of Veterans Affairs is investigating the unusual pattern of lung-related diseases in veterans from these wars [Iraq and Afghanistan]" (2012). Another article published by Burn Pit Claims Blogspot, May 20, 2011, reports on new studies being conducted "connecting the respiratory illness of troops returning from Middle East deployment to their exposure to toxic dust and fumes from 'burn pits.'"

Senior Airman Frances Gavalis tosses unserviceable uniform items into a burn pit on March 10 at Balad Air Base, Iraq. Military uniform items must be burned to ensure they cannot be used by opposing forces, according to the US military. Photo credit: Photo by U.S. Air Force/Senior Airman Julianne Showalter

Breathing dust, fumes, and other toxic substances from burn pits, exposed troops, contractors, and civilians deployed overseas to serious health hazards. Some of the chemicals were *very toxic carcinogens and are deadly*.
Photo credit: Grossman Attorneys. (2012)

Visit the online report by PBS Newshour: Photo Essay: The burn pits of Iraq and Afghanistan, produced by Dan Sagalyn November 17, 2014, for more disconcerting pictures of burn pits contaminating the surroundings of our veterans on base as well as civilian communities.

Water

Water quality in Iraq has also been questioned as many soldiers have experienced serious symptoms connected with exposure to sodium dichromate, an anticorrosion agent, while guarding an Iraqi water treatment plant. This dust, some believe, was not in the water but was scattered around the water treatment site prior to the American troops' arrival. While this was not potable water, exposure of the guarding soldiers walking in the dust potentiated the risk of developing cancer (Master, 2009).

In the award-winning moving *The Hurt Locker,* (2008) directed by Kathryn Bigelow, the Special Forces in Iraq were shown defusing roadside bombs, the IEDs. Throughout the movie, the soldiers drank their water from plastic bottles. Perhaps the only contamination from their drinking water was phthalates. Phthalates are components that soften plastics. Accumulated levels become endocrine disruptors distorting normal gene signaling, which can affect fertility in sperm, create cancers, and develop autoimmune disorders. They can also exhibit "feminization" traits in males (studies exist showing this occurrence in amphibians) and asthmatic conditions (freedrinkingwater.com, 2012).

Phthlates not only exist in the bottled water provided to protect soldiers from drinking foreign water with contaminants they are not accustomed to, but soldiers also often eat food from plastic trays and cups. These items are then included in the trash contents that cause further exposure to toxic contaminants as breakdown components when they enter the burn pits. Inhalation of the toxic release of styrene and dioxins from burning plastics can "aggravate respiratory ailments such as asthma and emphysema, … [and can cause] damages in the nervous system, kidney or liver" according to information provided by Women in Europe for a Common Future (WECF) (2012).

Bathing in untreated water creates another problem for veteran exposure to contaminants that can infiltrate cuts and wounds with pathogens as well as any other chemical contaminants leaching from area groundwaters.

The following photo is included to show not only the concern for having clean water for soldiers to prevent gastrointestinal reactions and other responses to phthalates (plastics) contamination, but to also reflect that bottled water may not be in the best interest of soldiers in this environment. Perhaps the solution is to provide a portable high-tech water treatment/purification operation as an essential component of operations in foreign lands to avert the additional contamination from plastic containers and exposures to burning plastic toxins.

This picture depicts bottled water arriving from Kuwait.
Photo credit: Science energy.gov.

This information reflects only a handful of toxic exposures experienced daily by veterans serving in Iraq and Afghanistan. Consider the liver trying desperately to keep up with the onslaught of chemical exposures and the adrenal glands rallying every hour to enable a soldier to meet the demands of the war mission.

However, one must not overlook the challenge facing soldiers with their daily diet in the combat zone. Pre-packaged meals are distributed to veterans leaving base for patrols. These foods have a long shelf life and contain many additives presently known to not be conducive to physical and mental health. While it can be easily understood that this food distribution program may be the best available, and it is understood that the military has taken great strides in researching and developing combat zone feeding operations to meet the caloric and energy expenditure needs of soldiers, one must become aware of the consequences of this type of long-term low-nutrient ingestion.

Military Meals—Harmful Ingredients to Mental/Emotional Well Being

Food additives, colorants, dyes, stabilizers, emulsifiers, and artificial hormones added to food products have been shown to cause depression (Rogers, 1997a). These ingredients influence brain activity. Aspartame, an artificial sweetener 180 times sweeter than table sugar, "can cause marked blood increases of phenylalanine, a substance linked to addictive eating patterns" (Rogers, 1997a). The aspartic acid in aspartame is considered an "excitotoxin," an amino acid responsible for "exciting" the brain into higher action. Its counterpart would be calming amino acids such as tryptophan.

Glutamate is another amino acid found naturally in the brain that excites brain function. As in all things, overly high levels of glutamate can create a cascade of negative, unwanted brain responses as serious as seizures. Monosodium glutamate (MSG), a popular food flavor enhancer, when consumed often raises the amount of glutamate available to the brain and can overexcite its transmitting responses.

As the public began to recognize the negative impact of MSG, product manufacturers began disguising MSG under other names, such as "hydrolyzed vegetable protein, vegetable protein, natural flavorings, spices" (p. 34) to name a few, according to Russell Blaylock, MD (1997), in his book, *Excitotoxins: The Taste that Kills.* Blaylock reports that scientific studies by Dr. John W. Olney revealed his discovery that "not only did MSG cause severe damage to the neurons in the retina of the eye, but that it also caused widespread destruction of neurons in the hypothalamus and other areas of the brain" (p. 35). When levels of excitotoxins, such as aspartate and glutamate, rise to high concentrations from constant ingestion, "they become deadly toxins" to the brain causing cells to "degenerate and die" (p. 39).

Yellow dye number 5 is another toxin to brain chemistry. This dye is part of orange, red, and green food colorants and is known as tartrazine. This dye is used to make foods look better or to look as if they contain eggs. "Tartrazine can lower zinc levels that affect brain functions utilizing zinc creating depression or hyperactivity" (Rogers, 1997a). All food additives, flavor enhancers, colorants, and texturizers are included in processed foods to enhance flavor and to cause one to think the foods are healthy. Many additives also extend the shelf life of a food, something most consumers value in their busy lives without realizing the harmfulness and lack of nourishment these additives create. Considering the military needs to provide quick and easy meals for millions of soldiers in extreme environments, shelf life is a critical component for feeding operations. However, it takes good nutrients to detoxify these non-nutritious ingredients, and over time it can create a vital nutrient depletion situation, which in turn affects brain health.

MREs—Meals Ready-to-Eat—Military Provisions

"The Military Nutrition Division at the U.S. Army Research Institute of Environmental Medicine (USARIEM, 2012) has been at the forefront of research to address the psychological, physiological, and nutritional requirements of modern military personnel" according to Military Nutrition.com (2011). This group of researchers collaborates with other institutions such as "Tufts University, the USDA, Massachusetts Institute of Technology, and Brigham and Women's Hospital" to address the nutritional needs of soldiers in extreme conditions to sustain "warfighter health, resilience, cognitive and physical performance, and survivability." This organization, while under the direction of Dr. Andrew Young and Mr. Gerry Garsch, developed a four-part program focusing on the following areas:

1. Metabolic Regulators to Optimize Warfighter Performance to metabolically regulate physiological functions affecting performance and susceptibility to illness, infection, and injury;

2. Nutritionally Optimized First Strike Ration to determine the optimal levels of macro and micro-nutrients for sustaining soldier cognitive and physical performance, and especially focuses on formulating "on-the-move" nutrient delivery systems;

3. Weight Management programs;

4. Combat Ration Sustainment Testing Program that evaluates and/or improves rations from records of soldiers in training or deployed to combat zones (2011).

MREs are totally self-contained meals. Soldiers may be issued one or three meals a day dependent upon their orders and for how long they may be away from the main base and operational kitchens. These meals are "designed to withstand rough conditions and exposure to the elements" as referenced by MREInfo.com (2010). The prepackaged meals contain an entrée providing many choices, such as spaghetti, beef stew, vegetables with pasta, chicken, and burritos, a side dish such as corn, fruit, and/or potatoes, crackers or bread, a spread such as peanut butter, jam, or cheese, dessert, candy, beverages that are Gatorade-like, flavored drink mixes such as lemonade, cocoa, dairy shakes, coffee, or tea, a seasoning packet such as hot sauce, a self-contained unit for heating the food, often a flameless device, and the necessary accessories such as napkins, spoons, matches, sugar, salt, pepper, creamer, chewing gum, and toilet paper. One providing company even includes a postcard recycled from the cardboard container for the soldiers to complete to send home (USARIEM, 2012).

The following photos show the meal packages and some of the actual food contents.

Photo credits: MREInfo.com website, retrieved March 13, 2012.

The shelf life of the MREs is approximately "three (3) years at 80 degrees F" according to Preparedness Advice Blog (2012). However, they report that with proper refrigeration or cold storage, that time frame could be extended. Several companies provide MREs to the military, and each one has developed their menu plans that provide different caloric values. Below is a chart of the main providers and their individual meal values:

Co. Name	Location	Amount of Calories
Sopakco	Mullins, SC	900–1250
AmeriQual	Evansville, IN	1410–1460
MRE Star	Arden, NC	1100–1300
Epicenter	Eugene, OR	850–1450

Differences may be due to some packs not containing all three daily meals, such as omitting breakfast, gum, candy, etc.

I compared three packaged meals as listed by AmeriQual Company: the Vegetable Stew with Beef, Southwestern Style Chicken with Black Beans & Rice, and Pasta with Garden Vegetables in Tomato Sauce. I listed in Excel spreadsheet format only the ingredients that appeared to be additives, flavorings, some vitamin additives, and dyes. I did not list the generally recognized foods such as the beef, chicken, or vegetables, although I feel in this prepackaged format, these food items are lower in nutrient value at best.

The general menu plan for the three meals is as follows:

Vegetable Beef Stew	Chicken/Beans/Rice	Pasta/Vegetables
Entrée	Entrée	Entrée
Choc. chip cookie	Choc. chip cookie	Oatmeal cookie
Toaster Pastry	Toaster Pastry	Toaster Pastry
w/brown sugar	w/brown sugar	w/brown sugar
Peanut butter	Peanut butter	Peanut butter
Cracker	Cracker	Cracker
Lemonade flavor drink mix	Lemonade flavor drink mix	Lemonade flavor drink mix
Raisins		
Spoon, towelette	Spoon, towelette	Spoon, towelette
Heater	Heater	Heater
Salt water for heater	Salt water for heater	Salt water for heater

The code, P, C, or B on the left side of the chart below references the pasta, chicken, or beef meal. I have listed the ingredient list of additives as well as what they do for the food, such as serve as thickener, emulsifier, color stabilizer, texturizer, or sweetener. I have also made notations about some of the negative and nutritionally harmful effects of such additives, especially when consumed daily, that can cause undue stress on the physiological systems of the body. The four most important and damaging ingredients to brain function are the: (1) aspartame—in the lemonade drink, (2) MSG in the form of modified corn starch, modified food starch, and autolyzed yeast extract, (3) highly processed corn oil, soybean oil, and cottonseed oil, and (4) yellow #5 tartrazine dye.

MRE Comparing Pasta, Chicken, and Beef Meals

P	C	B	Ingredient	Action
	X	x	modified corn starch	thickening agent, stabilizer, emulsifier, treated with HCL acid, not healthy, not harmful
		x	sodium phosphate	meat preservative
x		x	modified food starch	thickening agent, stabilizer, emulsifier, treated with HCL acid, not healthy, not harmful
x	X	x	erythorbic acid	preservative, vegetable derived from sucrose, antioxidant in processed foods
x		x	autolyzed yeast extract	flavor enhancer, and MSG derivative (free glutamic acid)
		x	hydrolyzed soy protein	flavor retention
x	X	x	caramel color	made from sucrose, may help prevent oxidation in bottled beverages
		x	flavorings	no description of actual ingredients in "flavorings"
		x	corn oil	generally hydrogenated, possible GMO
x	X	x	partially hydrogenated and fully refined soybean oil	generally GMO, increases trans fats, rancid from light and processing
		x	mono & di glycerides	fats generally made from oils, emulsifiers, texture, to prevent separation
		x	sodium benzoate	Preservative, kills bacterial yeast and fungi, not considered a carcinogen except with vitamin C
x	x	x	artificial flavors and colors, colored with beta carotene	beta carotene provides orange coloring, more natural food colorant, provides some pro-vitamin A as antioxidant
		x	vitamin A palmitate	naturally occurring vitamin in animal sources and manufactured synthetically

P	C	B	Ingredient	Action
x	x	x	partially hydrogenated soybean and cottonseed oil	generally GMO, increases trans fats, rancid from light and processing
	x	x	Dextrose	a sugar
		x	Vanillin	artificial flavor
		x	powdered eggs	dried and pasteurized eggs, highly processed product
x	x	x	high fructose corn syrup	starch derivative, sweetener
x	x	x	sodium acid pyrophosphate	buffering, cheleating, GRAS, maintains color
x	x	x	monocalcium phosphate	leavening agent, also used in fertilizers
		x	Niacinamide	Vitamin B3, GRAS
x	x	x	thiamin mononitrate	Vitamin B1, GRAS
x	x	x	TBHQ and citric acid	for freshness, chemical preservative, form of butane, delays onset of rancidity, many side effects
		x	Gelatin	protein thickener and stabilizer
x			pyridoxine hydrochloride	Vitamin B6
x	x	x	thiamin hydrochloride	Vitamin B1, nutrient enhancer
x	x	x	rapeseed, cottonseed and soybean oils	generally GMO, increases trans fats, rancid from light and processing
x	x	x	calcium carbonate	maintains white food colors, controls acidity
x	x	x	sodium citrate	buffer to control pH, emulsifier
x	x	x	aspartame	artificial sweetener, toxic, excitotoxin especially to the brain
x	x	x	acesulfame potassium	artificial sweetener
x	x	x	tricalcium phosphate	anticaking, raising agent, used in fertilizers also
x	x	x	yellow number 5	food colorant, excitotoxin
x	x	x	phenylketonurics **	contains phenylalanine, synthetic aspartame

Considering all the exposures experienced by soldiers in theaters of war and understanding how the body works and what it needs to maintain optimal brain and body system functions, it becomes clearer the need for inclusion of nutritional intervention as part of a veteran's recovery program

Returning Home—the Road to Recovery

Notification of the end of one's deployment must come with mixed emotions for soldiers. First, joy at the thought of returning to loved ones, extended family, friends, and even pets stateside fills the heart and energizes all expectations. But there may also exist a second feeling of loss, a sense of separation from the family structure of one's troop mates, the intensity of one's job, and the importance of each soldier's participation in the military objective. The sense of "aliveness and purpose" may continue to run strongly in the veins of all soldiers and then become coupled with the enthusiasm of "finally returning home."

The alarming and rising statistics reporting suicide among some returning veterans begins to paint a very different picture of a truly happy homecoming, a picture of troubled memories and self-perceptions, guilt, shame, remorse, confusion, loss of one's newfound self with military buddies, and fulfilling exciting and unprecedented personal and military objectives juxtaposed with an inability to fit back into old traditional societal and family patterns when the reality of war situations scatters over every aspect of one's thoughts, remembrances, and home front activities. Recognition of the overall depletion of biological, physiological, emotional, and psychological reserves offers a direction for not only "bringing our soldiers back home," but also bringing them back to life.

Our society has become so used to fast foods and grab-and-go meals. We just don't think twice about incorporating these quick fixes into our busy routines. Most of it really tastes good too; that's why we return to these foods often. It is easy to understand a veteran desiring to experience again his Big Mac with double fries and supersized cola! It represents a taste of home, albeit a pretty low-nutrition meal.

For all returning soldiers, it becomes essentially important to educate them on the importance of replenishing their bodies with wholesome foods and the reasons why fast food should not be initially considered. The information above describes the downward spiral of nutrient depletion occurring in combat zones from high levels of toxic exposures, their ingestion of packaged MREs for their on-the-go maneuvers, as well as the potential for their not having available fresh foods often enough to replenish their nutrient needs at other times at established mobile kitchens.

The following five-step nutrient replenishment plan, including the adoption of a whole foods diet, detoxification protocols, appropriate supplementation, exercise, and spiritual time for self with massage therapy, meditation, yoga, and/or time in nature, will begin the replacement of vital nutrition to depleted bodies and will support brain function and cellular signaling essential for communication patterns to the hypothalamus, the pituitary, the adrenal glands, the thyroid, the liver, the gastrointestinal system, and the immune system—the important players orchestrating vital health, well-being, and mental stability. It offers an easy-to-follow plan for spouses/partners that will not be overwhelming or difficult to incorporate into existing family routines.

Step 1: Integrate a Whole Foods Diet

What exactly is a whole foods diet? To many people, any food represents whole food. It's food! But whole foods are different from processed or refined foods, packaged foods, or most fast foods that are cooked in such a way as to render their nutrient value quite low.

Whole foods are foods that have all of their nutrient constituents intact. For example, a raw carrot contains all of the vitamins and minerals it generates during its growth and development. Whole grains, raw seeds and nuts, and legumes all contain the nutritious properties they garner from the soils and sunlight. When we ingest whole foods, we receive the benefit of all the component parts of these plant foods that nurture our own bodies. Whole foods include raw fruits, vegetables including the dark green leafy ones, whole grains, nuts, seeds, and legumes (peas, beans), as well as pasture-raised meat, free-range poultry, dairy products, and deep, cold-water fish such as salmon, mackerel, and sardines.

In contrast, refined foods go through manufacturing processes that remove many vital nutrients, such as wheat processing removing the vital and nutrient rich "germ," using a bleaching agent to develop a flour product that is white, deodorizing processes to eliminate rancidity factors, and adding thickeners and fillers to create a consistency and texture that is appealing to consumers. Often vital ingredients that were removed are "re-fortified"—that is replaced, but often with lesser grade and/or chemical derivatives of the nutrient removed by processing. Most processed/refined foods also contain chemical additives for color and flavor enhancement and for adding longevity for the food "product" on the shelves of markets. Many food products today have undergone genetic modification (GM) and may present numerous problems leading to allergic-type responses.

Therefore, it is vitally important to include whole foods in the diet for veterans to begin the replenishment process for all their cellular functions.

Below is a chart reflecting people's nutrient needs, some foods containing those nutrients, and some of the benefits of those foods for supporting the hypothalamus, pituitary, and adrenal glands—the first critical players in cellular signaling for stress management and organ system management.

Organ/Gland[1]	Nutrient	Foods Containing	Some Beneficial Actions in Body
Hypothalamus	Vitamin A	dark greens, colorful veggies, egg yolks, dairy	antioxidant, blood, bones, vision
	Biotin	brewer's yeast, peas, oats, walnuts, seeds, brown rice, Swiss chard, cooked eggs, almonds	gluconeogenesis, fatty acid synthesis; low causes nervous system impairment, depression, lethargy
	EFA	fish, fish oils, borage oil, flaxseed oil	cellular membrane structure
	Minerals	grains, nuts, seeds, green leafy vegetables, legumes	bones, muscles, organs, energy production, stress
Pituitary	Proteins	meats, whole foods, plants, legumes, seafood	provides amino acids required by pituitary
	Vitamin E	eggs, organ meats, leafy greens, almonds, wheat germ	protects cell membranes, antioxidant, lowers cholesterol, improves CV system, improves immune, function, needs zinc and selenium
	Manganese	citrus fruits, whole grains, green leaves, egg yolk, all fish—salt water is best	controls blood sugar, regulates thyroid hormones, addresses fatigue, free radical damage, allergies, sprains, strains
Adrenals	B5	organ meats, fish, poultry, milk, whole grains, legumes, nuts, eggs, broccoli, oranges, berries, potatoes, tomatoes, yogurt, mushrooms	energy metabolism, synthesis of lipids, neurotransmitters, steroid hormones, hemoglobin; low causes restlessness, irritability, GI distress, neurological distress, apathy, insomnia

[1] Chart Resources: Krystle Shapiro, compilation nutrient charts, Drs. Lam, et al at Tuberose.com (Adrenal Supporting Foods), Braun at Ezine Articles (Pituitary Supporting Foods).

Organ/Gland[1]	Nutrient	Foods Containing	Some Beneficial Actions in Body
	B6	cantaloupe, bananas, cabbage, greens, organ, meats, whole grains, salt water fish	amino acid metabolism, energy production, helps thinking and logic, immune function, steroid hormone activity; low causes depression, confusion, abnormal brain waves
	Vitamin C	Cabbage family, black currants, kale, parsley, citrus, red and green bell peppers	antioxidant, helps form collagen, converts tryptophan, assists in hormone production, adrenal function, stress, heavy metal exposure, smoking; when low it causes depression
	Zinc	red meat, oysters, fish, nuts, seeds, ginger, artichokes, blackberries, almonds, squash, eggs, cucumbers, yogurt	Needed for enzyme systems, cell mediated immunity, mental development, protein synthesis, blood sugar control, DNA synthesis, for thymus function.
	Magnesium	tofu, whole grains, nuts, seeds, legumes, leafy greens, kale, collards, baked potato with skin, spinach, oats, brown rice	brain, muscles, fluids, kidney, liver, energy production, calcium uptake, heart and blood pressure, cramp relief, appetite, fatigue, mental processing; low causes irritability
	Potassium	potatoes, tomatoes, avocados, bananas, plant foods, fish, asparagus, broccoli, carrots, celery, corn, beans, seaweeds, Swiss chard, chicken, salmon	balances fluids, regulates blood pressure, improves adrenal and kidney function, calming, balances pH

This list provides a reference to many necessary foods and makes it easy to recognize the convenience of whole foods becoming a part of one's daily diet and why they are important to health. Menu plans also can easily be designed from this partial list of foods supporting mental health and well-being.

Incorporating a whole foods diet may have some challenges for some veterans if their digestion is faulty. Therefore it may be necessary to improve their digestive functions in the beginning. As referenced earlier, brain function requires efficient digestion to receive the necessary nutrients for effective cellular signaling. According to Elizabeth Lipski, PhD, in her book, *Digestive Wellness* (2004), signs and symptoms of digestive irregularities may include problems with gums such as gingivitis creating "irritation and inflammation in the mouth" (p. 173), belching and gastric reflux, low output of hydrochloric acid, or even excessive output. One might also experience nausea, vomiting, flatulence, bloating, constipation, diarrhea, indigestion, stomach pains, or cramps (Lipski, 2004) and feelings of a lack of energy following meals—suggesting a potential malabsorption problem.

Allergies and/or food sensitivities may be present and must be addressed. Recognition of these foods and removing them from the diet will be an important step in improving digestion as well as other uncomfortable experiences like sinus irritations, fatigue, irritable skin conditions, achy joints, depression, or respiratory challenges. A food elimination diet provides you with the opportunity to recognize food triggers setting off such reactions. The most common food triggers are wheat/gluten, eggs, soy, many grains, dairy, corn, peanuts, refined foods, artificial sweeteners and flavor enhancers, and some meats, such as shellfish, beef, and pork. Corn and soy products are often included in processed animal feed that then becomes a part of the animals' tissues. A food elimination diet helps to recognize possible triggering foods. It is important to keep a journal of foods eaten and any sensations or experiences one has following ingestion. Then the process begins to eliminate those foods, often one by one, to see if symptoms subside. Once one is symptom free, introduce a potential triggering food one at a time to see if symptoms recur. If so, then one knows there is an allergy to that food. It takes time, but overall it is worth it to recover from food allergy symptoms and heal. A holistic nutritionist can provide the guidelines for succeeding with an elimination diet.

Supplements may be necessary to jump start the system now receiving good whole foods but needing support to utilize them. Good intestinal flora is important for proper breakdown of foods. These include live cultures in pre- and probiotics such as lactobacillis and bifidobacillis. Enzyme support may be necessary with the inclusion of digestive bitters, such as dandelion root tea. And most importantly for returning soldiers is the need to include a high-quality antioxidant product to begin to chelate and remove heavy metal toxicity, airborne toxins, and any other toxic chemicals accumulated while in the service. Vitamins E and C, selenium, N-acetyl cysteine, zinc, manganese, copper, Co-enzyme Q10, lipoic acid, and superoxide dismutase (Lipski, 2004, p. 89) all support repair and recovery of digestive linings and activity. More information on supplements will be discussed in step 3, supplementation.

Another component of step 1, whole foods, will be learning better cooking methods to preserve the wholesome nutrients. Elimination of fried foods, cooking foods with low temperature, steaming foods, and the use of the right oils and fats for cooking will greatly enhance food and flavor appeal as well as digestion.

Including raw foods, such as vegetable salads, fruit smoothies, and fresh fruit and vegetable juices, in meals more often will increase nutrient density and enhance health.

Step 2: Detoxification

A primary need for veterans is to focus on detoxification of the myriad detritus of accumulated chemicals, as referenced earlier, that cause dysfunction in communication between the brain and the body and that can lead to misperceptions of thought and mood disorders as well as physical ailments.

The liver undertakes the majority of detoxification activities; however, Jacqueline Krohn, MD, with Frances Taylor, MA, in their book *Natural Detoxification* (2000), report that detoxification actions also occur in the lungs and kidneys and some lesser activities occur in the "intestines, adrenal cortex, testes, spleen, heart, muscles, brain, and skin" (p. 34). It is easy to recognize how the body cells, which are active every moment metabolizing and creating energy, need support in getting rid of the sludge of cellular life.

Phases of Detoxification

Detoxification occurs in two phases. A brief discussion will clarify basic detoxification actions and the important nutrients required for energy production to keep things going and to provide the raw materials to carry out elimination processes.

Phase I detoxification involves breaking down chemicals in a harmful state to a non-harmful state. This is a preparation phase. Many chemicals are not water soluble and are therefore difficult to eliminate through the kidneys. Phase I begins the breakdown process by many steps removing something such as a sulfur group or an amino group or adding something such as oxygen or hydrogen. "At least 50 enzymes in 10 families governed by 35 different genes allow Phase I to take place" (Krohn & Taylor, 2000, p. 33).

Phase II detoxification takes over adding other chemical groups to render the toxins water soluble to be eliminated by the kidneys or bile. This phase also takes many steps and requires essential nutrients generating energy to function. "The efficiency of Phase I and Phase II is adversely affected by deficiencies of vitamins, minerals, amino acids, and fatty acids" (Krohn & Taylor, 2000, p. 36).

The following chart reflects the nutrient needs of both phases and foods providing the necessary raw materials. It is easy to see from the chart alone how valuable it is to design one's diet to include a variety of foods and that most of the foods reflected on the chart are familiar and easy to incorporate into a daily/weekly menu plan. Further, understanding the importance of such a nutritious approach for properly feeding veterans to improve their mental as well as physical health and to overcome any arising suicidal ideation hopefully motivates families as well as the veterans to be diligent in improving their health and well-being through eating true food.

Nutrients[2]	Phase I Nutrient Needs
Vitamins	
Vitamin A, Beta-carotene	red, yellow, green vegetables
Vitamin B1, Thiamin	dairy, meats, legumes, whole grains, nuts
Vitamin C	fruits, green vegetables, tomatoes
Vitamin E	vegetable oils, green leafy vegetables, milk, eggs, nuts, whole grains
Minerals	
Copper	meat, seafood, nuts
Iron	beans, meats, dark green vegetables
Magnesium	nuts, legumes, dark green vegetables, beans
Manganese	leafy vegetables, whole grains, nuts, bananas, beans
Molybdenum	whole grains, legumes, seeds
Sulfur	garlic, eggs, onions, meats, beans
Zinc	shellfish, meats, dairy, pumpkin seeds, beans, spinach
Other Nutrients	
Choline	whole grains, cheese, legumes, meats
Fatty Acids	flaxseed, soybeans, fish oils
Lecithin	legumes, grains, eggs, fish
Methionine	meat, eggs, whole grains
Oils	flaxseed, evening primrose, black currant seed
Silymarin	milk thistle

---

[2] Jacqueline Krohn and Frances Taylor, *Natural Detoxification*. Pt. Roberts, WA: Hartley & Marks Publishers, Inc., 2000.

Phase II Nutrient Needs	
Vitamins	
Folic acid	dark leafy vegetables, cabbage family, organ meats
Vitamin B1, Thiamin	dairy, meats, legumes, whole grains nuts
Vitamin B2, Riboflavin	milk, meat, dark green leafy vegetables
Vitamin B3, Niacin	meat, eggs, poultry, fish, whole grains
Vitamin B5, Pantothenic acid	nuts, meats, whole grains, green vegetables, potatoes
Vitamin B6, Pyridoxine	meats, vegetables, whole grains, green leafy vegetables, potatoes
Vitamin B12, Cobalamin	meat, dairy products, eggs, spirulina, chlorella
Vitamin C	fruits, green vegetables, tomatoes
Minerals	
Germanium	garlic, shiitake mushrooms, onions
Magnesium	nuts, legumes, dark green vegetables, beans
Manganese	leafy vegetables, whole grains, nuts, bananas, beans
Molybdenum	whole grains, legumes, seeds
Selenium	brewer's yeast, garlic, liver, eggs
Sulfur	garlic, eggs, onions, meats, beans, cheese, peanuts
Zinc	shellfish, meats, dairy, pumpkin seeds
Other Nutrients	
Cysteine	eggs, meats, onion family
D-glucarate	Vegetables
L-glutathione (reduced)	produced in body from cysteine, glutamic acid, and glycine
N-acetyl-cysteine (NAC)	taken as supplement—precursor to glutathione, converted to cysteine
Taurine	meats, seafood

Adopting a whole foods diet will begin the detoxification process without much ado for veterans who need to rest and not undertake any complicated programs or procedures. In more serious situations where a veteran may require medical intervention, then those protocols will certainly dominate.

Benefits of Far Infrared Sauna (FIR) for Detoxification

The far infrared (FIR) sauna provides another healthy way to detoxify. Far infrared waves, part of the light spectrum, are natural and familiar to the human body. While we do not perceive FIR as color, we experience it as heat—a heat wave that can penetrate into the body about one to one and a half inches. The heat causes the body to sweat; toxins are fat soluble and are attracted to the moving sweat. Once sweat is on the skin, it becomes imperative to wipe it off quickly to avoid reabsorption, especially when exiting the sauna. Dr. Sherry Rogers (2001b) points out the importance of understanding that some vital nutrients, like magnesium and salts, are also released in sweat and need to be replenished when one uses a FIR sauna regularly. She itemizes the importance of balanced multiminerals, multivitamins, fatty acids, phosphotidyl choline, CoQ10, carnitine, and other nutrients that are important and amounts depend "on the individual's diet, environments, diseases, and other parameters" (p. 187). She also points out that a FIR sauna "stimulates endorphins or happy hormones of the brain and kill[s] organisms like bacteria and parasites" (p. 171). Increasing the level of happy hormones supports improvement in thought processes that could discourage suicidal thoughts.

Another important detoxification strategy involves supplementation with antioxidants. Foreign toxins, chemicals, and even toxic wastes from cellular metabolism create damage to body tissues by becoming unstable molecules that flit throughout the system, seeking stability by adding electrons. Antioxidants undertake the responsibility of attaching and/or surrounding such unstable molecules and rendering them harmless or stabilizing them with their own electrons, which in turn can mean that the antioxidant becomes an oxidant—a damager. When the diet consists of lots of vitamins and minerals providing antioxidant materials, this is a small problem and is usually balanced overall. For the returning veteran, antioxidant supplementation along with their whole foods diet may become vitally important in restoring health. Step 3 discusses specific supplements and antioxidants important for healing and for supporting brain health to prevent deterioration and the potential for depression and suicidal ideation.

Step 3: Supplementation

Returning from combat might bring about mixed feelings as well as confusion once life at home with family resumes. The last thing a veteran needs is to face a complicated dietary and supplement regimen even though he/ she will benefit from such helpful recovery support. Deciding upon the most appropriate supplementation must include many factors: the veteran's understanding of the need to replenish lost nutrients and his/her willingness to undertake a recovery program including improving diet, detoxification practices, exercising regularly, and taking care of oneself in the ways discussed earlier. Just including a few key supplements may make a huge difference in feeling like oneself again physically, psychologically, and emotionally.

But how does one choose supplements that will be most effective in overcoming existing health conditions and ensuring overall improvement? A first step might begin by ordering an Organic Acids Test (OAT). This urine analysis test provides an overview of a person's compromised metabolic functions, such as yeast or bacterial overgrowth, nutritional deficiencies, toxic load levels, or effects of drugs, both medicinal and recreational, on cellular activities. This information can begin to paint an individualized picture of important changes necessary to restore one's ability to function physically and psychologically.

The test is easy to interpret and provides suggestions for supplements based on the individualized OAT findings. It may recommend dietary changes, specific nutrient supplements, antioxidants (that support detoxification and immune system activities), and cellular metabolism needs for energy production.

Metabolic dysfunction, as stated above, often leads to mood disorders, emotional irregularities, fatigue, erratic behavior, digestive disorders, and challenges with maintaining ideal weight.

You can check online for these two laboratories that provide the organic acids test: Metametrix and Genova.

I have provided the chart below listing several supplements that support digestion, detoxification, liver function, and immune system activities. Along with a whole foods diet, considering supplement suggestions on this list that match with your OAT recommendations will enable the body as well as the mind to return to normal physiological balances and energy production. It is important to note that each veteran is biochemically unique and presents with differing levels of stress residue and toxicity. A professional health care provider and/or holistic nutritionist will be able to establish the most appropriate supplements to consider and begin and determine optimal dosages based on individuality and the levels of toxicity, gastrointestinal disturbances, mood/anxiety discomforts, and any irregular sleep patterns. As well, many supplements may be discontinued as healing occurs.

Supplement[3]	How It Is Used by the Body
Pre-probiotics	may be necessary for digestive support and to restore good flora for intestines
Multivitamins/ Multiminerals	provides full complement of vitamins and minerals to fill in and/or ensure optimal nutrients

Supplement[3]	How It Is Used by the Body
Folic acid along with B12	protein metabolism, supports immune function, increases energy, brain function, improves digestion, supports detoxification methylation in phase II pathway, always take with balanced B-complex vitamins B12, maintains nerve myelin sheaths, improves energy, relieves irritability, improves memory
SAM	supports methylation, neurotransmitters, low in depressed patients, increases serotonin, dopamine, improves neurotransmitter binding to receptor sites
5-HTP	increases serotonin levels, increases endorphins, easily crosses blood brain barrier for improving mood
	Do not take with any other antidepressant drugs.
B-Complex	all aid in detoxification, need to be taken together for best results, for antibody production, cell respiration, stabilizing blood glucose levels, helps produce stomach hydrochloric acid, helps control cholesterol levels, supports detoxification processes
Botanicals	
St. John's Wort	improves symptoms of anxiety, depression, sleep disturbances, insomnia, apathy; select extract containing 0.3 percent hypericin and 3 percent to 5 percent hyperforin for best results
Milk Thistle	helps prevent oxidative stress to the liver
Essential fatty acids	1 tablespoon daily of deep cold-water fish oil or 1 tablespoon flaxseed oil to increase Omega 3 fatty acids, especially DHA and EPA
Vitamin C	antioxidant support—water soluble
Vitamin E	antioxidant support—fat soluble
Resveratrol	Antioxidant, anti-inflammatory, found in grapes, cranberries, peanuts
Quercetin	Support bioavailability of Resveratrol, a flavonoid, support for fatty liver
Betaine	Donor to methyl groups (detoxification), helps lower cardiovascular disorders, slows fat infiltration in liver

---

[3] Jacqueline Krohn, *Natural Detoxification*, 274–76. Joseph Pizzorno, et. al, *Textbook of Natural Medicine*, specific topics. Thorne Research, *Nutritional Support for Metabolism and Health Aging*, 2016.

Step 4: Exercise

Military training programs focus on developing strong, vibrant, physically fit, and resilient soldiers to meet the grueling demands of service, especially in combat arenas. The Marine Corps considers "the habits of self-discipline required to gain and maintain a high level of physical fitness … inherent to the Marine Corps way of life and must be a part of the character of every Marine" according to Stew Smith (2012b), personal trainer for the military writing for Military.com. Their physical fitness tests (PFT) include pull-ups, abdominal crunches, and a three-mile run.

The air force utilizes four tests: "aerobic (running), body-composition, push-ups, and crunches" (Smith, 2012c). The army requires a three-event physical performance test, including "two minutes of push-ups, two minutes of sit-ups, and a timed 2 mile run" (Smith 2012a).

Each group establishes criteria based on gender, age, amount of repetitions, and/or time elapsed and may include consideration of one's body composition.

These are rigorous standards undertaken by soldiers and are necessary to maintain during deployments to remain physically fit. Once soldiers return home, it becomes important to continue physical fitness activities to maintain health and also in support of detoxification and regaining nutritional balance.

The health benefits of exercise are many. Krohn and Taylor (2000) itemize the benefits physically as well as mentally and emotionally. Below is a list of some of these benefits, especially ones that support mental health, one of the biggest targets for preventing suicidal ideation (p. 328).

Physical Benefits	Mental/Emotional Benefits
Increases toxin removal	Improves overall mental health
Increases circulation—blood, lymph	Releases endorphins/elevates mood
Improves HDL (cholesterol levels)	Relieves depression
Lowers blood pressure	Improves self-image/self-confidence
Improves endurance/strength	Improves mental abilities
Increases strength, muscle tone	Decreases anger and hostility
Improves bone structure	Reduces tension and anxiety

Exercise provides another important benefit—improving digestion and cellular metabolism by increasing the amount of oxygen to cells necessary for energy production and cellular metabolism. David B. Agus, MD (2011), researching the increasing number of articles on the benefits of exercise, uncovered a 2009 study reflecting "evidence that exercise causes your brain to boost production of certain chemicals known to have antidepressant effects" (p. 227). He further describes how this research discovered that exercise excited a gene for a nerve growth factor called VGF. VGFs are small proteins critical to the development and maintenance of nerve cells, which further links exercise to brain health and the prevention of dementia and Alzheimer's disease. (p. 227)

Support of nerve growth becomes vitally important in the recovery processes of returning veterans having every system of their body tested and compromised and ready for remediation.

Many forms of exercise can be undertaken. The most important necessity, especially for veterans, is to get moving again. Walking or running regularly, joining a gym, or undertaking a favorite sport such as tennis, wrestling, golf, or swimming all contribute to the benefits listed above and to feelings of self-worth. Hiring a personal trainer to organize the optimal training progression upon returning may instill stronger motivation and follow through, which in turn delivers benefits to mental health. Having a personal trainer at one's side may also provide a sense of "buddy connection" to replace that sense of loss of one's military unit.

Yoga exercises come in many forms, and veterans may enjoy the rest, relaxation, skill building, and flexibility yoga provides. Yoga encourages people to focus on their thoughts and to become aware of their bodies and their movements. Yoga may provide rest from any ongoing military experience mind chatter disturbing one's ability to relax, let go, and move forward in life.

Step 5: Spirituality, Mindfulness, Mind-Set, and Mental Health

Mental health and well-being must include strengthening one's spiritual side. Participation in combat, confronting ideologies opposing one's own, separation for long periods of time from family and friends, and experiencing difficulty in returning to one's established routines can undermine one's sense of self and purpose. Suicide is the ultimate sense of loss of purpose and worth. For many, as the rising statistics have shown, finding their path back to their true selves proved too difficult an emotional task.

Beginning the replenishment of lost nutrients by incorporating a whole foods diet is an important step forward for supporting proper brain and organ systems functions. This alone may avert the onset of suicidal thoughts. Moving forward with detoxification protocols and beginning an exercise program all contribute to clearing thinking and improving one's sense of one's real self.

Mindfulness classes may also provide strong support for retraining veterans about how their thoughts and feelings, mind chatter, and wartime memories may be negatively coloring their perceptions and how they can learn to manage such patterns, often reframing the incoming thoughts to more appropriate ones. It is well known that what we think about all day long, we tend to become. Dwelling on negative feelings drives one toward negative behaviors and loss of self-worth. Being mindful of the running dialogue in one's head and learning to let go what is harmful, reframing thoughts into a more manageable and understandable reality, and utilizing the lessons to be gained from one's experiences, even the most horrific ones, might become a most useful undertaking. To reframe means placing a more effective value on one's most troubling experiences. With a different and more positive value, one can relax and grow forward.

Massage therapy offers the opportunity for a veteran to reconnect with his or her own body. Massage is nurturing and supports detoxification, relaxation, digestion, and overall balanced health. Many types of energy work exist to assist in rebalancing the physical system and reducing physical and mental pain and distress. Following long deployments where a soldier is "on alert" twenty-four hours a day, massage therapy and body work offer a chance for soldiers to reconnect to the reality of their bodies, not their wartime bodies.

Reconnecting with natural surroundings most often is profoundly healing. Breathing in the clean, fresh air in the mountains, standing by streams and waterfalls, and taking in the presence, sights, and sounds of the ocean rejuvenate body, mind, and spirit. Who doesn't love a walk in the woods? Or being by the ocean sinking one's feet into wet sand, feeling the soft surf bubble around our ankles with the calls of gulls overhead seeking their daily sustenance? Taking time to revisit our own American landscapes enables veterans to reconnect with their own roots and to begin dissolving the harsh residues of their combat experiences.

Understanding and Taking Action

Every war draws a nation closer together or farther apart depending upon one's experiences and perspectives: a history of family members participating or succumbing to wars or a personal ideology for or against the ethics or politics of war. What stands ever present is the aftermath our soldiers experience—PTSD, depression, self-mutilation/harm, drug abuse, traumatic brain injuries, loss of limbs, and suicide that becomes terribly difficult for civilians to comprehend. Our long-standing wars in Iraq and Afghanistan have captured the attention of the world with the rising statistics of suicide by returning veterans. So many of us stand helplessly by, uncertain of how to make a difference other than to just love them. Love isn't enough if it still takes them by suicide. Understanding the biochemistry of the human body, its vital requirements, and how to effectively and promptly replenish such essential nutrition upon their return must stand out as a foremost approach for turning the tide of rising suicide in the aftermath of our current and most treacherous wars.

Leaders from all branches of the military as well as leadership in the Department of Defense must understand what physically occurs with the body under extreme stress, causing depletion of vital nutrient stores in bones, muscles, tissues, organs, and cells and how this affects brain health and mood. This knowledge must then lead to incorporating programs for all returning veterans to educate them on such a negative nutrient cascade and toxic accumulation occurring during their deployment(s), and then must train and motivate them to undertake effective replenishment of whole foods to regain their optimal health and mental and emotional well-being. Stringent protocols for end-of-deployment debriefings need to be as important as the strict standards each soldier must meet in preparation and fitness at the beginning of their training to manage the rigorous demands of all war efforts with physical strength, resilience, and quick thinking processes. Establishing the requirement of a few weeks at home bases dedicated to nutrient replenishment endeavors prior to returning to families is most important for recovery. Families want healthy soldiers returning, not unhealthy ones.

Using the information outlined above as educational materials for developing military protocols and educating veterans, their families, their medical teams, as well as community members supporting our returning troops will serve to reduce the number of veteran suicides and perhaps even to eliminate such behavior that leaves us all with deep and heartfelt sadness.

I wish to leave the following tribute to our American soldiers but also extend the same appreciation to all allied soldiers around the world who bravely face the unknown yet uphold the principles of their countries to ensure civil rights and personal freedoms for all.

Tribute to our American soldiers and veterans and to all the allies dedicated to preserving peace, democracy, and a true sense of brotherhood.

America By Edgar A. Guest

God has been good to men. He gave
His Only son their souls to save,
And then he made a second gift,
Which from their dreary lives should lift
The tyrant's yoke and set them free
From all who'd throttle liberty.
He gave America to men---
Fashioned this land we love, and then
Deep in her forests sowed the seed
Which was to serve man's earthly need.

When wisps of smoke first upwards curled
From pilgrim fires, upon the world
Unnoticed and unseen, began
God's second work of grace for man.
Here where the savage roamed and fought,
God sowed the seed of nobler thought;
Here to the land we love to claim,

The pioneers of freedom came;
Here has been cradled all that's best
In every human mind and breast.

For full four hundred years and more
Our land has stretched her welcoming shore
To weary feet from soils afar;
Soul-shackled serfs of king and czar
Have journeyed here and toiled and sung
And talked of freedom to their young,
And God above has smiled to see
This precious work of liberty,
And watched this second gift He gave
The dreary lives of men to save.

And now, when liberty's at bay,
And blood-stained tyrants force the fray,
Worn warriors, battling for the right,
Crushed by oppression's cruel might,
Hear in the dark through which they grope
America's glad cry of hope:
Man's liberty is not to die!
America is standing by!
World-wide shall human lives be free:
America has crossed the sea!

America! The land we love!
God's second gift from Heaven above,
Builded and fashioned out of truth,
Sinewed by him with splendid youth
For that glad day when shall be furled
All tyrant flags throughout the world.
For this our banner holds the sky:
That liberty shall never die.

For this, America began:
To make a brotherhood of man.

Making the Commitment

Changing dietary habits may be a difficult undertaking for returning veterans and their families. Many people do not have good eating habits to begin with. The influence of advertising, the convenience of processed and packaged foods, the demands on time for young families with small children, the slowdown of the economy stretching every dollar earned, and the need for quick fixes, whether it comes from fast foods, convenient foods, or restaurant foods, have become a normal way of life. Just watching what people purchase at the grocery checkout line proves this point. But another most important point is that many people just do not know what is good food versus what is bad food. They are driven by cost, convenience, and flavor. That is why it becomes essentially important to reeducate our veterans and their families, those who have sacrificed and struggled for our country's philosophy of freedom for all, to understand the importance of optimal nutrition and how to achieve great health and mental/emotional well-being through diet, exercise, detoxification, and being present with oneself.

Using the charts above and learning the importance of creating meals that incorporate a wide variety of the foods supporting brain and organ health will encourage families to eat well and be fully nourished. The sample meal ideas below serve as a guide and can be adjusted according to personal preferences.

It is my sincere wish that this information educates and encourages veterans and their families to take charge of their health. Just as the military forces establish pertinent fitness guidelines for maximum performance to meet the challenges of military objectives, families need to adopt pertinent nutritional guidelines and goals to ensure optimal health and positive, happy thinking for themselves, their children, and their most precious civil servants, our veterans.

Food preparation is really an act of love as well as an art. Cookbooks of every variety abound to inspire us and to teach us new concepts about feeding ourselves with such plans as vegetarian diets, macrobiotic diets, weight loss diets, and special diets for diabetes, arthritis, and cardiac conditions. New fad diets surface, like the Mediterranean diet, the Paleo diet, the new Atkins diet, the DASH diet, and the South Beach diet. How does one choose what is best?

Each person is so chemically individual and has experienced specific exposures due to a chosen lifestyle or circumstances, such as the high toxic environment in theaters of combat. A healthy dietary plan must consider such experiences, along with heredity, present conditions and/or illnesses, and personal choices, such as alcohol and/or tobacco consumption, levels of stress in family, community, and employment opportunities in selecting the proper nutritional approach for recovery and healing. Professional nutritional consultants will best be able to design the most effective course for nutrient replenishment. If one chooses to follow the guidelines provided above, a strong recovery process will begin as well.

Listed below are some basic instructions for including foods often not considered in one's diet. However, these foods provide many valuable nutrients for healing bodies. We live in a time when so many people, due to their busy multitasking lives, have drifted away from some very basic steps in food preparation, such as our ancestors once practiced.

The following foods provide hearty amounts of proteins, amino acids, vitamins, minerals, and fibers supporting overall health. Learning to prepare them properly and incorporating them into one's diet often will promote health and mental well-being.

Beans (Pulses)

Dried Form

Wash beans well, picking out any broken beans and pieces that float. Soak them overnight in cold water, leaving plenty of room for expansion. Drain and rinse them, and then cover them again with fresh cold water and boil rapidly for ten to fifteen minutes to remove toxins. Then reduce heat and continue cooking them for about one to one and a half hours until they are tender. Individual bean varieties may take longer, so check the package directions. Adzuki and mung beans may require shorter soaking times.

Cooking times

Black beans	One hour
Adzuki beans	Thirty-five to forty minutes
Navy beans	One to one and a half hours
Red kidney beans	One to one and a half hours
Pinto beans	One to one and a quarter hours
Garbanzo beans	One to one and a half hours

Note: do not salt during cooking or add any acidic foods, such as tomatoes, as this toughens them. Add them at the end of cooking.

Preparing beans ahead of time and storing in the refrigerator is quite helpful as beans can be added to salads, soups, and stews and provide a rich source of vitamins, minerals, fiber, and proteins.

Lentils and Peas

These legumes do not require presoaking and offer a rich variety of textures and flavors to many meals. It is best to rinse them first; then cook them according to the package directions, about twenty to thirty minutes depending on variety.

Lentil varieties: red, yellow, green, brown

Peas: yellow, green

Grains

Try a variety of grains, including wheat, rye, oats, millet, amaranth, bulgur, couscous, and quinoa. These grains can be added to salads, soups, or stews or eaten as hot cereal. Eliminate any gluten grains (wheat, rye, oats, spelt, kamut) if you are gluten sensitive.

Rice

Many varieties of rice are available. Experiment with all types to find your favorites. Brown rice, wild rice, red rice, and long-grain rice contain richer nutrients than processed white rice. Flavor rice with seasonings and herbs of your choice to provide taste variety as well as nutrients.

Seeds and Nuts[4]

Most seeds and nuts improve their flavor when roasted in a dry skillet. Place them in a skillet and roast them for two to three minutes over medium heat. These can be added to salads, yogurt, or soups, or just consumed as part of one's snack foods. Keep them refrigerated, but they are best used freshly roasted.

sesame seeds	sunflower seeds	poppy seeds
pumpkin seeds	hemp seeds	almonds
walnuts	chestnuts	pecans
cashews	pine nuts	Brazil nuts

---

[4] Information on beans, pulses, peas, grains, rice, seeds, and nuts selected from Nicola Graimes, consultant editor, *Complete Vegetarian*. London: Anness Publishing Ltd., 2006.

Fats and Oils, Cooking and Flavoring

The oils we use for cooking become vitally important as an improper cooking process can render fats and oils toxic and potentially carcinogenic. Frying often creates free radicals, which are unstable molecules that create damage to cellular walls and tissues. Most people love fried foods, including their crispy texture and the flavor; however, frying and deep frying of food creates several health-harming ingredients. By using specific oils that are tolerant of higher heat temperatures, one can enjoy richly flavored foods by sautéing rather than frying.

Do Not Use for Cooking

Fresh, refined, essential fatty acid rich seed oils such as flax, hemp, sunflower, or sesame oils should not be used.

Okay to Use for Cooking—Mostly Low Heat

Butter, coconut oil, palm oil, *high oleic* sunflower or safflower oils (not the regular ones), sesame oil, or olive oil can be used.[5] (Although I recommend these oils still be cooked at lower and slower temperatures. Note: once an oil has "smoked" in the pan, it is ruined. It must be discarded, the pan thoroughly cleansed, and the process started over.)

A better method is to sauté with water or broth first and then use the oils at the end for flavor. More broth can be added as needed. Broth contributes to making a nice sauce and prevents overheated oil spoilage.

Below is a chart that can be used for weekly planning to ensure that each family member eats a variety of foods each week to maximize nutrient intake.

---

[5] Udo Erasmus, *Fats That Heal, Fats That Kill*. Summerton, TN: Alive Books, 1993.

Weekly Food/Menu Planner[6]

Food Item	Mon	Tue	Wed	Thu	Fri	Sat	Sun
Grains							
Wheat							
Amaranth							
Brown rice							
Buckwheat							
Millet							
Oatmeal							
Quinoa							
Rye							
Wild rice							
Barley							
Dairy							
Eggs							
Cheese							
Cottage cheese							
Kefir							
Milk/buttermilk							
Sour cream							
Yogurt							

[6] Ellie Whitney and Sharon Rady Rolfes, *Understanding Nutrition*. Belmont, CA: Thomson Wadsworth, 2008.

Food Item	Mon	Tue	Wed	Thu	Fri	Sat	Sun
Legumes							
Beans—variety							
Peas							
Meats							
Beef							
Turkey							
Chicken							
Fish/seafood							
Bacon							
Lamb							
Liver or organ meats							
Fruit							
Apples							
Apricots							
Avocado							
Bananas							
Blackberries							
Blueberries							
Cantaloupe							
Cherries							
Grapefruit							
Grapes—green and red							
Mangoes							

Food Item	Mon	Tue	Wed	Thu	Fri	Sat	Sun
Nectarines							
Oranges							
Peaches							
Pineapple							
Plums							
Raisins							
Raspberries							
Strawberries							
Watermelon							
Vegetables							
Acorn squash							
Artichokes							
Beets							
Bell peppers—red, yellow, and green							
Broccoli							
Brussels sprouts							
Butternut squash							
Cabbage—green or purple							
Carrots							
Cauliflower							
Celery							
Cilantro							
Collard greens							

Food Item	Mon	Tue	Wed	Thu	Fri	Sat	Sun
Cucumbers							
Garlic							
Kale							
Leeks							
Lettuces							
Mushrooms							
Onions							
Parsley							
Russet potatoes							
Spaghetti squash							
Spinach							
String beans							
Sweet potatoes							
Swiss chard							
White or red potatoes							
Yams							
Yellow squash							
Zucchini							
Nuts/Seeds							
Sesame seeds							
Sunflower seeds							
Pumpkin seeds							
Walnuts							

Food Item	Mon	Tue	Wed	Thu	Fri	Sat	Sun
Almonds							
Cashews							
Pecans							
Flaxseeds							
Oils							
Extra virgin olive oil							
High oleic sunflower oil							
High oleic safflower oil							
Coconut oil							
Fish oil							
Borage oil							
Black currant oil							

Servings Recommended Per Day based on a 2,000-calorie diet

Grains	6 oz.	breakfast cereals, on salads, in soups/stews
Fruits	2 cups	with breakfast, as snacks, on salads, in smoothies, as dessert
Vegetables	2 1/2 cups	fresh, raw, steamed on salads, as side dish, with pasta
Seeds	small handful	sprinkle on salads, in soups, or consume fresh raw for snacks
Nuts	small handful	sprinkle on salads, in soups, or consume fresh raw for snacks
Meats/legumes	5 1/2 oz.	breakfast, lunch, dinner, on salads, in soups, stews

References

Agency for Toxic Substances & Disease Registry (ATSDR). *Benzene*. Retrieved January 18, 2012, from http://www.atsdr.cdc.gov/substances/ toxsubstance.asp?toxid=14

Agency for Toxic Substances & Disease Registry (ATSDR). *Toluene*. Retrieved January 18, 2012, from http://www.atsdr.cdc.gov/substance/toxsubstance.asp?toxid=29

Agus, MD, David B. (2011). *The end of illness*. New York: Free Press.

Airgas. Material Safety Data Sheet: *N-butane*. Retrieved January 18, 2012, From http://www.airgas.com/documents/pdf/001007.pdf

Alphdisability.com. (2010, September 10). *Burn pits suspected as cause for respiratory illness and disability*. Retrieved January 15, 2012, from http://www.alphadisability.com/burn-pits-suspected-as-cause-for-respiratory-illness-and-disability/

Altman, Howard. (2011, May 18). Tampa Bay Online. *Senators press for burn pit update from military*. Retrieved January 18, 2012, from http://www2.tbo.com/search/?source=all&query=burn+pits

Ameriqual. *Military meals ready to eat*. Retrieved February 17, 2012, from http://www.ameriqual.com/military/individual _rations.php

Blaylock, Russell L. (1997). *Excitotoxins, the taste that kills*. Albuquerque, NM: Heath Press.

Braun, Lucia. *The influence of the pituitary gland on your body*. Retrieved December 1, 2011, from http://ezinearticles.com/?The-influence-of-the- pituitary-on-your-body&id-838447

Brauser, Deborah. (2011, August 26). *Low DHA levels linked to increased suicide risk*. Retrieved December 31, 2011, from http://www.medscape.com/viewarticle/748615_print

Burnpitclaims.com. (2011, May 20). *US senators request update on regulations to protect soldiers from burn pit toxins*. Retrieved January 15, 2012, from http://www.burnpitclaimsblogspot.com/2011/05/us-senators-request-update-on.html

Clayman, MD, Charles. (Ed). (1995). *The human body book*. New York: DK Publishing.

Consumer Support Group (CSG Network). *Aviation jet fuel information*. Retrieved February 17, 2012, from http://www.csgnetwork.com/jetfuel.html

Cuciureanu, Magdalena D. & Vink, Robert. (2011). *Magnesium and stress*. Retrieved March 21, 2012, from http://www.adelaide.edu.au/press/titles/magnesium/magnesium-ebook.pdf

Eby III, George A., Eby, Karen L., & Murck, Harald. (2011). *Magnesium and major depression*. Retrieved March 21, 2012, from http://www.adelaide.edu.au/press/titles/magnesium/magnesium-ebook.pdf

Environmental Bureau of Investigation (EBI). (2012). *Benzene. human health*. Retrieved March 21, 2012, from http://www.e-b-i.net/ebi/contaminants/benzene.htm

Epicenter. *MRE military meals ready to eat.* Retrieved February 17, 2012, from http://www.theepicenter.com/mre_military_meal_ready_to_eat.htm

Erasmus, Udo. (1993). *Fats that heal, fats that kill.* Summerton, TN: Alive Books

Franklin Institute. *The human brain: low-level noise and stress-research.* Retrieved February 8, 2012, from http://www.fi.edu/learn/brain/stress.html

Freedrinkingwater.com. *Endocrine disruptors. environmental toxins in drinking water: phthalates.* Retrieved March 20, 2012, from http://www.freedrinkingwater.com/water_quality2/envtoxin-phthlates-quality.htm

Fuchs, Nan Kathryn. (2002). *Basic health publications user's guide to calcium & magnesium.* Laguna Beach, CA: Basic Health Publications, Inc.

Fuel-Testers. *What is gasoline? The composition of gasoline.* Retrieved February 17, 2012, from http://www.fuel-testers.com/what_is_gasoline_e10.html

Garcia, J. Malcolm. (2011, August 24). *Toxic trash: the burn pits of Iraq and Afghanistan. Smoke Signals.* Retrieved January 18, 2012, from http://www.oxfordamerican.org/articles/2011/aug/24/smoke-signals/

Graimes, Nicola, (Ed). (2006). *Complete vegetarian.* London: Hermes House.

Greenblatt, James M. (2011, September 8). Psychology Today. *The breakthrough depression solution.* Retrieved January 5, 2012, from http://www.psychologytoday.com/blog/the-breakthrough-depression-solution/201109/nutritional-risk-factors-suicide

Guest, Edgar A. (1934). *Collected verse of Edgar A. Guest.* America. Chicago: The Reilly & Life Co.

Harrell, Dr. Margaret C., & Berglass, Nancy. *Losing the battle: the challenge of Military suicide.* Retrieved January 16, 2012, from http://www.cnas.org/files/documents/publications/CNAS_LosingTheBattle_HarrellBerglass.pdf

HealthAliciousNess.com. *Top 10 foods highest in beta carotene.* Retrieved March 21, 2012, from http://www.healthaliciousness.com/articles/natural –food-sources-of-beta-carotene.php

Heller, Jacob L. *Toluene and xylene poisoning.* Updated February 3, 2010. Retrieved February 17, 2012, from http://www.nlm.nih.gov/medlineplus/ency/article/002829.htm

Kalmus, Sage. 2011. *Herbs and foods for pituitary gland function.* Retrieved January 17, 2012, from http://www.livestrong.com/article/478536-herbs-foods-for-pituitary-gland-function/

Katz, David A., (1998). *Food Additives: What they do.* Retrieved February 10, 2012, from http://www.chymist.com/food%20additives-what%20they%do.pdf

Krohn, Jacqueline, & Taylor, Frances. (2000). *Natural detoxification.* Pt. Roberts, WA: Hartley & Marks Publishers, Inc.

Lam, MD, Michael, Schmitt, Dr. Walter, & Wilson, Dr. James L., *The adrenal glands: endocrine support products.* Retrieved January 17, 2012 from http://tuberose.com/adrenal_Glands.html

Lipski, Elizabeth. (2005). *Digestive wellness.* New York: McGraw Hill

Lombard, Dr. Jay, & Germano, Carl. (1997). *The brain wellness plan*. New York: Kensington Press.

McLaughlin, August. (2011). *Food for the pituitary gland*. Retrieved January 17, 2012, from http://www.livestrong. com/article/485023-food-for-the-pituitary-gland/

Menna, Amy. (2011) *Suicide and the military*. Retrieved December 31, 2011, from http://psych.central.com/ lib/2011/suicide-and-the-military/3/

Military Nutrition.com. *Modern Military Nutrition Research, 1986—Present*. Retrieved November 29, 2011, from http://www.military-nutrition.com/eras/1986 to Present.aspx

MREinfo.com. *MREs (Meals, Ready-to-Eat)*. Retrieved February 2, 2012, from http://www.mreinfo.com/us/ mre/mres/html

MRE Star. *MRE meals*. Retrieved February 17, 2012 from, http://mre-meals.net/

Pizzorno Jr., Joseph E., & Murray, Michael T. (2006). *Textbook of natural medicine*, (3rd ed.), (Vols 1 & 2). St. Louis: Churchill Livingstone Elsevier.

Preparedness Advice Blog. (Posted March 17, 2011). Retrieved March 13, 2012 from http://preparednessadvice. com/foodstorage/336/

Rogers, Sherry A. (1997a). *Depression cured at last*. New York: SK Publishing.

Rogers, Sherry A. (2001b). *Pain free in 6 weeks*. Sarasota, FL: Sand Key Company, Inc.

Rohrer, W. Jean. *The pituitary gland a "master gland"*. Retrieved January 17, 2012, from http://webnat.com/article/ Pituitary.asp

Schmidt, Ph.D, Michael A. (2007). *Brain building nutrition*. Berkeley, CA: Frog Books.

Science Lab.com. Material Safety Data Sheet, *Kerosene MSDS*. Retrieved January 18, 2012, from http://www. sciencelab.com/msda.php?msdsld=9924436

Smith, Stew. *Army basic training PFT*. Retrieved March 3, 2012, from http://www.military.com/fitness-center/ military-fitness/stew-smith/archive

Smith, Stew. *Marine corps physical fitness test*. Retrieved March 3, 2012, from http://www.military.com/ fitness-center/military-fitness/stew-smith/archive

Smith, Stew. *USAF fitness program*. Retrieved March 3, 2012, from http://www.military.com/fitness-center/ military-fitness/stew-smith/archive

Sopakco. *Military meals*. Retrieved February 2, 2012 from, http://www.Sopakco.com/military_meals

Stone, Martin. (2006). *Liver health, a natural approach*. Orem, UT: Woodland Publishing.

University of Maryland Medical Center. (2012). *Trans fats 101*. Retrieved March 15, 2012, from http://www.umm. edu/features/transfats.htm.

USARIEM. (2012). *Nutrient delivery system*. Retrieved February 17, 2012, from http://www.usariem.army.mil/ pages/images/Marketing_PDFs/NDSFlyerLR.pdf

U.S. Department of Veterans Affairs, (2016) Suicide Among Veterans and Other Americans 2001—2014. Office of Suicide Prevention. Updated August 3, 2016 by the Office of Mental Health and Suicide Prevention.

Van der Kolk, Bessel A., McFarlane, Alexander C., & Weisaeth, Lars, (Eds). (2007). *Traumatic stress: the effects of overwhelming experience on mind, body, and society.* New York: The Guilford Press.

Whitney, Ellie, & Rolfes, Sharon Rady. (2008). *Understanding nutrition* (11th ed.). Belmont, CA: Thomson Higher Education.

Whole Grains Council. (2012). *Whole grains-an important source of essential nutrients.* Retrieved March 18, 2012 from http://wholegrainscouncil.org/whole-grains-101/whole-grains-an-important-source-of-essential-nutrients

Wickedroots.com. *Neurotoxic effects from butane gas.* Retrieved March 21, 2012 from, http://www.wickedroots.com/Vaporizers/neurotoxic-Effects-Butane-Gas.html

Wikipedia. (2012a). *Stress (biology).* Modified January 24, 2012. Retrieved February 17, 2012, from http://en.wikipedia.org/w/index.php?title=Stress_(biology)&oldid=473048813

Wikipedia. (2012b). *Ethanol.* Retrieved February 17, 2012, from http://en.wikipedia.org/wiki/ethanol

Wikipedia. (2012c). *Naptha, health hazards.* Retrieved February 17, 2012, from http://en.wikipedia.org/wiki/naptha health hazards

Wikipedia. (2012d) *NMDAR receptor.* Retrieved February 17, 20012, from http://en.wikipedia.org/wiki/NMDA_receptor

Wikipedia. (2012e) *Tetraethyllead.* Retrieved February 18, 2012, from http://en.wikipedia.org/wiki/tetraethyllead

Women in Europe for a Common Future. (2004-2005). *Dangerous health Effects of home burning of plastics and waste.* Retrieved March 22, 2012, From http://www.wecf.eu/cms/download/2004-2005/homeburning_plastics.pdf.

Wong, Kristina. (2011, November 2). *New report: military losing the battle against suicide.* Retrieved 12/31/2011, from http://abcnews.go.com/blogs/politics/2011/11/new-report-military-losing-the-battle-against-suicide/

Wong, Kristina. (2011, September 27). *Rising suicides stump military leaders.* Retrieved December 31, 2011, from http://abcnews.go.com/US/rising-suicides-stump-military-leaders/story?id.14578134

Zukier, Z., Solomon, Jessse A., & Hamadeh, Mazen J. (2011, April). *The role of nutrition in mental health: suicide.* Retrieved December 31, 2011, from http://www.mindingourbodies.ca/about-the-project/literature_reviews/suicide_and_nutrition

Photo Credits

Burn pits:

Altman, Howard. (2011, May 18). The Tampa Bay Tribune. *Senators press for Burn pit update from military.* Retrieved January 15, 2012 from http://www2.tbo.com/search/?source=all&query=burn+pits

(Girl tossing clothing into burn pit)

Grossman Attorneys. *Our defense base act lawyers help contractors injured in Iraq and Afghanistan.* Retrieved January 15, 2012 from http://grossmanattorneys.com/pages/defense-base-act.html?gclid=cluGv4: hq64CFSUOQgodAxEVRw
(field burning site showing burnt metal, truck, and towers in background)

Water truck

Science energy.gov. *Water truck arriving from Kuwait.* Retrieved January 15, 2012, from http://science.energy.gov/news/in-focus/2011/06-23-11/

Feeding Operations/MREs

Department of Defense. (2012). Food service equipment & field feeding Systems. Retrieved February 17, 2012, from http://nsrdec.natick.Army.mil/media/print/FSE_3ED.pdf

9/19

CPSIA information can be obtained
at www.ICGtesting.com
Printed in the USA
LVHW072252090819
627208LV00010B/12/P

9 781489 719003